American Council for
The United Nations University

The Millennium Project

2004 State of the Future

JEROME C. GLENN AND THEODORE J. GORDON

*The **State of the Future 2004** contains very valuable information for humanity and leaders throughout the world that cannot be found elsewhere.*

Dr. Horacio O'Donnell, Chancellor
Universidad de Ciencias Empresariales y Sociales, Argentina

*I assure you that I and my colleagues at the United Nations find the **State of the Future**'s annual guidance invaluable.*

Michael Doyle, UN Assistant Secretary-General and
Special Advisor to UN Secretary-General Kofi Annan

Five of the last seven annual *State of the Future* reports were selected by *Future Survey* as among the year's best books on the future.

ISBN: 0-9722051-2-8   Library of Congress Control Number: 2004108659

© 2004 American Council for the United Nations University
   4421 Garrison Street, NW
   Washington, D.C. 20016-4055 U.S.A.

The Millennium Project is the sole responsibility of the American Council for the United Nations University. It is not directed by the United Nations University headquartered in Tokyo, Japan, nor is it currently sponsored by or part of the UNU's research program.

by Jerome C. Glenn and Theodore J. Gordon

Cover Design and Cover Photography by Norbert Conrad, Germany
www.art-beat.de

Print Section—Table of Contents

The *2004 State of the Future* is composed of two parts: print and CD. This print book contains the executive summary of each of the studies conducted in 2003–04. The enclosed CD of over 3,000 pages contains the cumulative work of the Millennium Project since 1996 and details of the studies included in this print section. See the next page for the contents of the CD.

See next page for the Table of Contents of the CD.

CD Section—Table of Contents

See preceding page for Table of Contents of the Print Section

The enclosed CD of over 3,000 pages contains the cumulative work of the Millennium Project since 1996 and details of the studies included in this print section.

Millennium Project Node Chairs

The Millennium Project interconnects global and local perspectives through its Nodes (groups of individuals and institutions). They identify knowledgeable and creative people in their region, translate questionnaires, conduct interviews, and disseminate the project's findings. The Node Chairs are:

Australasia
Paul Wildman
The Futures Foundation
Brisbane, Australia

Brazil
Arnoldo José de Hoyos
and Rosa Alegria
São Paulo Catholic University
São Paulo, Brazil

Brussels-Area
Philippe Destatte
The Destree Institute
Namur, Belgium

Central Europe
Pavel Novacek
Charles University
Prague, Czech Republic

Ivan Klinec
Institute for Forecasting
Bratislava, Slovak Republic

China
Rusong Wang
Chinese Academy of Natural Sciences
Beijing, China

Zhouying Jin
Chinese Academy of Social Sciences
Beijing, China

Egypt
Kamal Zaki Mahmoud Sheer
Futures Research and Studies Center
Cairo, Egypt

France
Saphia Richou
Prospective-Foresight Network
Paris, France

Finland
Mika Aaltonen
Finland Futures Academy
Turku, Finland

Germany
Cornelia Daheim
Z_punkt GmbH The Foresight Company
Essen, Germany

Gulf Region
Ismail Al-Shatti
Gulf Institute for Futures and Strategic Studies
Kuwait, Kuwait

Iran
Mohsen Bahrami
Amir Kabir University of Technology
Tehran, Iran

India
Anandhavalli Mahadevan
Mother Teresa Women's University
Kodaikanal, India

Italy
Eleonora Barbieri Massini
Gregorian University
Rome, Italy

Japan
Shinji Matsumoto
CSP Corporation
Tokyo, Japan

Latin America
Miguel Angel Gutierrez
Center for Globalization and Prospective
Buenos Aires, Argentina

Eduardo Balbi
Escenarios y Estrategia—EYE
Buenos Aires, Argentina

Mexico
Concepción Olavarrieta
Nodo Mexicano. El Proyecto Del Milenio, A.C.
Mexico City, Mexico

Russia
Nadezhda Gaponenko
Future-Oriented Science and Technology
Russian Institute for Economy, Policy and Law
Moscow, Russia

Silicon Valley
John J. Gottsman
Clarity Group
San Francisco CA, USA

United Kingdom
Bruce Lloyd
South Bank University
London, United Kingdom

Venezuela
Jose Cordeiro
Sociedad Mundial del Futuro Venezuela
Caracas, Venezuela

Experimental Cyber-Node
Frank Catanzaro
Arcturus Research & Design Group
Maui, Hawaii

The Millennium Project of the American Council for the United Nations University was sponsored in its 2003–04 research program by:

- **Amana Institute, Brazil**
- **Applied Materials**
- **Army Environmental Policy Institute, U.S. Army**
- **Dar Almashora, for Kuwait Oil Company**
- **Deloitte & Touche**
- **General Motors**

with in-kind support from:

- **Smithsonian Institution**
- **World Federation of United Nations Associations**
- **World Future Society**

This report is the eighth in an annual series intended to provide a *context for global thinking* and improved understanding of global issues, opportunities, challenges, and strategies.

The purposes of the Millennium Project are to assist in organizing futures research, improve thinking about the future, and make that thinking available through a variety of media for consideration in policymaking, advanced training, public education, and feedback, ideally in order to accumulate wisdom about potential futures.

The project is designed to provide an independent, global capacity that is interdisciplinary, interinstitutional, and multicultural for early alert and analysis of long-range issues, opportunities, challenges, and strategies.

The Project is *not* intended to be a one-time study of the future, but to provide an on-going *capacity* as an intellectually, geographically, and institutionally dispersed think tank.

Feedback on this work is welcome and will help shape the next *State of the Future*.

Readers of the *State of the Future* may also be interested in the *Futures Research Methodology* Version 2.0 CD, which is a collection of 27 chapters about how to explore the future.

MILLENNIUM PROJECT PLANNING COMMITTEE

Olugbenga Adesida, President, The Knowledge Network, Cape Town, South Africa

Mohsen Bahrami, Amir Kabir University of Technology and Nat. Research Council of Iran, Tehran, Iran

Eduardo Raul Balbi, Scenarios & Strategies (Escenarios y Estrategia –EYE), Buenos Aires, Argentina

Eleonora Barbieri Masini, Pontifical Gregorian University, Rome, Italy

Peter Bishop, Program for the Study of the Future, University of Houston, Clearlake TX, USA

José Cordeiro, Sociedad Mundial del Futuro Venezuela, Caracas, Venezuela

George Cowan, Founder, Santa Fe Institute, Santa Fe NM, USA

Cornelia Daheim, Z_punkt GmbH The Foresight Company, Essen, Germany

Francisco Dallmeier, Biodiversity, Smithsonian Institution, Washington DC, USA

James Dator, University of Hawaii HI, USA

Nadezhda Gaponenko, Russian Institute for Economy, Policy and Law, Moscow, Russia

Jerome Glenn, AC/UNU Millennium Project, Washington DC, USA

Michel Godet, Conservatoire d'Arts et Métiers, Paris, France

John J. Gottsman, President, Clarity Group, Atherton CA, USA

Theodore J. Gordon, AC/UNU Millennium Project, Old Lyme CT, USA

Miguel A. Gutierrez, Latin American Ct for Globalization Studies & Future Res., Buenos Aires, Argentina

Hazel Henderson, Futurist, Author and Consultant, St. Augustine FL, USA

Arnoldo José de Hoyos Guevara, PUC-SP São Paulo Catholic University, São Paulo, Brazil

Zhouying Jin, Chinese Academy of Social Sciences, Beijing, China

Bruce Lloyd, South Bank University, Department of Futures Studies, London, UK

Anandhavalli Mahadevan, Vice Chancellor, Mother Teresa Women's Univ., Kodaikanal, Tamil Nadu, India

Pentti Malaska, Finland Futures Academy, Helsinki, Finland

Kamal Zaki Mahmoud Sheer, Cairo University, Cairo, Egypt

Shinji Matsumoto, President, CSP Corporation and Member, Japan Society for Future Studies, Tokyo, Japan

Pavel Novacek, Palacky University, Olomouc, and Charles University, Prague, Czech Republic

Concepción Olavarrieta, Nodo Mexicano. El Proyecto Del Milenio, A.C., Mexico City, Mexico

Charles Perrottet, Principal, The Futures Strategy Group, Glastonbury CT, USA

Cristina Puentes-Markides, Pan American Health Organization, Washington DC, USA

David Rejeski, Director, Foresight and Governance, Woodrow Wilson Center, Washington DC, USA

Saphia Richou, President, Prospective-Foresight Network, Paris, France

Stanley Rosen, Director, Strategic Planning, Boeing Satellite Systems, Los Angeles CA, USA

Saddig Salih, Senior Economist, Islamic Development Bank, Jeddah, Saudi Arabia

Mihaly Simai, Director, World Institute of Economics, Budapest, Hungary

Rusong Wang, Chinese Academy of Natural Sciences, Beijing, China

Paul Werbos, National Science Foundation, Arlington VA, USA

Paul Wildman, The Futures Foundation, Brisbane, Australia

Norio Yamamoto, Executive Director, Global Infrastructure Foundation, Tokyo, Japan

Sponsor Representatives

Oscar Motomura, President, Amana-Key, Brazil

Michael K. O'Farrell, Applied Materials, USA

John Fittipaldi, Army Environmental Policy Institute, U.S. Army

Ismail Al-Shati, Chairman and CEO, Dar Almashora, Kuwait

Michael Stoneking, Deloitte & Touche LLP, USA

Julie Blair, General Motors, USA

ACKNOWLEDGMENTS

The Millennium Project Node chairs and co-chairs, who select participants, translate questionnaires, and conduct interviews, were essential for the success of the research this year.

Theodore Gordon, Jerome Glenn, and Elizabeth Florescu were partners in the research through this volume, but special acknowledgment is given for Theodore Gordon's quantitative and conceptual leadership in the further development of the State of the Future Index, Jerome Glenn's leadership on the cumulative research on the 15 Global Challenges, and Elizabeth Florescu's research and organization of environmental security issues.

Special recognition goes to José Cordeiro and to Carlos Eduardo Bujanda Armas, Edgar Cotte, and Juan Lovera from Deloitte & Touche in Caracas for preparing the first national SOFIs presented in Chapter 4.

Cristina Puentes-Markides, Paul Werbos, Tom Murphy, John Young, Frank Catanzaro, José Cordeiro, and Concepción Olavarrieta contributed review and improvements to the text. Susan Jette contributed the additions to the annotated scenario bibliography in the CD.

The analysis and writing of Scenario 1 of the Middle East Peace Scenario Study in Chapter 5 was led by Jerome Glenn, and Theodore Gordon led the work on Scenarios 2 and 3. Special thanks to Kamal Zaki Mahmoud for initiating this study.

Principal members of the environmental security scanning team who prepared the monthly reports summarized in Chapter 6 were Elizabeth Florescu, Peter Rzeszotarski, John Young, Robert Jarrett, and Jerome Glenn.

Frank Catanzaro and Jerome Glenn produced the last chapter on the new Millennium Project Weblog Database.

Linda Starke provided editing of the print section. John Young provided proofreading assistance for several sections in both the print and CD sections.

Elizabeth Florescu did the production and layout of both the print and CD sections of this book under a very tight deadline. Norbert Conrad designed the cover and assisted with the artwork and layout of the print section.

Special acknowledgments go to the Millennium Project Interns who contributed to the general operations of the Millennium Project and the updating of the 15 Global Challenges: John Atkinson, Sahar Batman, Chetana Bisarya, Natasha Doulia, Amy Ekdawi, Misato Fujiki, Rosana Herrera Gálvez, Vassia Gueorguieva, Deborah R. Hupert, Ana Jakil, Hayato Kobayashi, Daniel Lucchesi, Carina McDonald, Dino Manalis, Kim Mikyeong, Lambrina Mileva, Lindsey Novom, Anu Patil, Andra Tautu, and Prachi Vaish. We wish them all well in their future careers.

Congratulations to the Kuwait Node for initiating futures research work with the Kuwait Oil Company and to the European Nodes for initiating futures research work with the European Union, and special thanks to the Brazil Node for help in organizing the Planning Committee Meeting in São Paulo.

FOREWORD

The purpose of futures research is to systematically explore, create, and test both possible and desirable futures to improve decisions. Decisionmaking is increasingly affected by globalization; hence, global futures research will be needed to inform decisions made by individuals, groups, and institutions.

Because the issues and solutions of our time are increasingly transnational, transinstitutional, and trandisciplinary, and because more and more people participate in decisionmaking than in the past, the Millennium Project was created as a global participatory think tank of futurists, scholars, scientists, business planners, and policymakers who work for international organizations, governments, corporations, NGOs, and universities.

Futures research has had an uncomfortable relationship with most academic research. As the latter advances, it tends to narrow its scope of study. In contrast, futures research tends to broaden its scope of study as it advances, to take into account future possibilities. It is not a science; the outcome of studies depends on the methods used and the skills of the practitioners. Its methods can be highly quantitative (such as the State of the Future Index in Chapter 3) or qualitative (such as the Delphis that produced the Middle East Peace Scenarios in Chapter 5). It helps to provide a framework to better understand the present and to expand mental horizons (such as the Global Challenges in Chapter 1).

The *2004 State of the Future* provides an additional eye on global change. This is the eighth *State of the Future* report. It contains the eight-year cumulative research and judgments of approximately 1,650 thoughtful and creative people. Nearly 250 people participated in last year's studies. The institutional and geographic demographics of the participants can be found in the Appendix, and full lists of participants are available in Appendix A on the CD.

The annual *State of the Future* is a utility from which people can draw information and ideas to be adapted to their unique needs. It provides a global strategic landscape that public and private policymakers may use to improve their own strategic decisionmaking and global understanding. Business executives can use the research as input to their scenario planning. University professors, futurists, and other consultants may find this information useful in teaching and research. Sections of previous reports have been used as university and high school texts.

The *2004 State of the Future* comes in two parts: a CD with complete details of the Millennium Project's research this year and over the past several years, and this print edition of a series of distilled versions of the 2003–04 research. Consider each chapter of the print part as the executive summary of each chapter in the CD. For example, the print Chapter 1 on the 15 Global Challenges allocates two pages to each Challenge, while the CD devotes nearly 600 pages to them.

The CD can also be used to search for just those items you might need to put together your own customized report. There are a range of regional views on each of the 15 Challenges. For example, all the African sections on each of the 15 Challenges could be assembled into one paper by cutting and pasting (and possibly adding to the content by searching for results on Africa in other chapters), providing one report on Global Challenges and Issues for Africa.

It is not expected that anyone will read the entire 3,000 or so pages of the CD version of the report. We believe, however, that people will search for key words and print specific sections of interest. In the CD, each Challenge has a more comprehensive overview, alternative views or additions to the overview, regional views and relevant information from recent literature, a set of actions from previous Global Lookout Panels with a range of views from previous interviews with decisionmakers augmented by new items and views over the past year, additional actions and views on those actions, and suggested indicators to measure progress or lack thereof on addressing the challenge.

The statements in the Global Challenges Chapter do not represent a consensus because they are a distillation of a range of views from hundreds of participants, rather than an essay by a single author. We sought and welcomed a diversity of opinions. Hence, some of the issues raised and recommended actions seem contradictory. In addition, there does not appear to be a cause-and-effect relationship in some of the statements, and some sound like political clichés, but these are the views of the participants that may be useful to consider in the policy process.

The Millennium Project's Nodes are groups of individuals and organizations that interconnect global and local perspectives. They identify participants, conduct interviews, translate and distribute questionnaires, and conduct research and conferences. It is through their contributions that the world picture of this report and indeed all of the Millennium Project's work emerges.

Through its research, publications, conferences, and Nodes, the Millennium Project helps to nurture an international collaborative spirit of free inquiry and feedback for increasing collective intelligence to improve social, technical, and environmental viability for human development. Feedback on any sections of the book is most welcome at <jglenn@igc.org> and may help shape the next *State of the Future*.

Jerome C. Glenn	Theodore J. Gordon	Elizabeth Florescu
Director	Senior Fellow	Director of Research
Millennium Project	Millennium Project	Millennium Project

What Is New in This Year's Report

♦ The Global Challenges in Chapter 1 were updated and improved via an international Delphi and environmental scanning by staff and interns.

♦ Progress measures for Global Challenges are presented in Chapter 2 with developments that could affect the variables in the State of the Future Index.

♦ Updated analysis for the new 2004 State of the Future Index, a work in progress, to measure the near-term future of the human condition.

♦ The first national SOFIs for selected countries of the Americas.

♦ Three Middle East Peace Scenarios based on a three-round unique Delphi.

♦ Scanning reports of emerging environmental security issues with implications for international agreements.

♦ A weblog database is being developed to broaden the input to update and improve the 15 Global Challenges and other future issues for next year.

♦ About 50 scenarios were added to the Annotated Scenarios Bibliography on the CD, for a total of over 550 scenarios or scenario sets.

♦ The CD includes details and supportive research of the print version and the complete text of previous Millennium Project works:

 • Global exploratory, normative, and very-long range scenarios, along with an introduction to their development.

 • Three Middle East Peace scenarios and the three-year study behind them.

 • Science and Technology scenarios and the two-year supporting study.

 • An analysis of the statements by world leaders delivered at the UN Millennium Summit in 2000.

 • Environmental security definitions, threats, related treaties; UN military doctrine on environmental issues; potential of military environmental crimes prosecuted by the International Criminal Court; changing environmental security military requirements in 2010–25; and factors required for successful implementation of futures research in decisionmaking.

 • Two studies to create indexes and maps of the status of sustainable development, conducted by the Millennium Project participants, and an international review of the concept of creating a "Partnership for Sustainable Development," a study initiated by the Central European Node.

EXECUTIVE SUMMARY

We may be in a race between the increasing proliferation of threats and our increasing ability to improve the human condition. This drama drives many people around the world to fight destructive fatalism by implementing innovations benefiting humanity. Yet the emergence of world conscience strategically focused on global challenges is too often distracted by trivia in the media, government pettiness, valueless marketing, daily complexities of survival, and all forms of information pollution. Nevertheless, enough wisdom has prevailed to accelerate human development for a growing majority of the world.

The insights in this year's *State of the Future* can help decisionmakers and educators who work to counter hopeless despair, blind confidence, and ignorant indifference—attitudes that too often have blocked efforts to improve the prospects for humanity. Last year's edition began with the statement:

> *After seven years of accumulative global futures research by the Millennium Project, it has become increasingly clear that humanity has the resources to address its global challenges; what is less clear is how much wisdom, good will, and intelligence will be focused on these challenges.*

This eighth year of the Project's work further confirms this conclusion. One of the greatest dramas is whether current and future efforts to achieve sustainable development will be sufficient to prevent global warming from seriously damaging civilization and life-support systems, eventually leading to a greenhouse effect growing beyond human control. Atmospheric CO_2 has gone up again for another record year, three of the last five years were the warmest in recorded history, and the world could use more than twice as much fossil fuels over the next 50 years as over past 50.

We face numerous other daunting challenges: water tables are falling on every continent, agricultural land is becoming brackish, groundwater aquifers are being polluted, 1.1 billion people do not have access to safe drinking water, and 2.4 billion lack adequate sanitation. By 2050 more than 2 billion people could be living in water-scarce areas, forcing masses of people to migrate into inhumane conditions. Without sufficient nutrition, shelter, water, and sanitation, it is reasonable to expect increased migrations, conflicts, and disease.

At the same time, millions of people around the world work daily to produce more intelligent human-nature symbioses. Although the interdependence of economic growth and technological innovation has made it possible for 3–4 billion people to have relatively good health and living conditions today, unless our financial, economic, environmental, and social behaviors are improved along with our industrial technologies, the long-term future could be more difficult. However, with cheaper materials and better automation we can easily cut inputs in half and double outputs; with better ICT we can more optimally match ideas, people, resources, and challenges worldwide in real time; with emerging global ethics and decision support systems, improved policies seem possible. But will this be sufficient to engage our thinking far enough into the future to get ahead of problems and seize opportunities?

The dynamics of urbanization coordinates with so many important improvements to the human condition that urbanization—once thought of as a problem—is now seen as part of the solution to poverty, ignorance, disease, and malnutrition.

By 2050 there could be 2 billion people who are 60 or older, which will be more than the number who are under 15. Assuming no major breakthroughs in life extension research, one UN alternative forecast projects that by the end of this century world population could actually be a billion lower than today. This would force changes

in retirement and in health care systems and cultures worldwide. Yet the current population of 6.4 billion is forecasted to grow to 8.9 billion by 2050; 98% of this growth is expected in the poorer countries. The North is suffering from aging, declining populations and the need to provide retirement benefits, while the South is suffering from growing populations with very limited opportunities. It seems that a global strategy to match these needs and resources should be on the international agenda.

The number of democracies is growing, the number of dictatorships is decreasing, and more people will vote this year then ever before in history. At the same time, there are approximately 50 failed nation-states. What are the international community's responsibilities for anticipating future failed states and rescuing current ones?

Globally oriented, future-oriented politicians are urgently needed. There is no escaping the need to educate the public, who could in turn elect more global future–minded politicians. The completion of the Human Genome Project, the Internet, AIDS, management of the International Space Station, globalization of the news media, and the evolution of the WTO, NATO, and the EU—all relatively unthinkable just 25 years ago—are some of the factors that demonstrate the acceleration, complexity, and globalization that are increasing the need for global, long-term perspectives in our decisionmaking. Yet graduate programs in global futures research are scarce.

Meanwhile, the merging of information and telecommunications technologies is creating a self-organizing mechanism that can improve the collective intelligence of humanity. As mobile phones and the Internet merge, China is set to become a unique cyber phenomenon: it has the largest number of mobile phone users in the world and within two years it will also have the most Internet users. As the integration of cell phones, video, and the Internet grows, prices will fall, accelerating globalization and allowing swarms of people to quickly form and disband, coordinate actions, and share information ranging from stock market tips to bold new contagious ideas (*meme epidemics*). About 13% of humanity connects to the Internet, and the digital divide is narrowing. At the same time, civilization is vulnerable to cyber terrorism, power outages, information pollution (misinformation, pornography, junk e-mail, media violence), and virus attacks. (The probability of a catastrophic attack—global damages in excess of $100 billion from a chain of combined events—has risen from 2.5% for 2003 to about 30% for 2004, according to mi2g Ltd.)

In the past 20 years, income per capita has grown almost 10%, life expectancy has increased about seven years, secondary school enrollments have grown by 30%, and infant mortality has dropped by almost 40%. Yet without major policy interventions, the income disparities could grow enough to create global instabilities. The ratio of the average income of people in the top 5% to the bottom 5% has grown from 6:1 in 1980 to over 200:1 now.

More than 30 new and highly infectious diseases have been identified in the last 20 years, such as avian flu, Ebola, AIDS, SARS, and cross-species viruses in Africa; for many there is no treatment, cure, or vaccine. The Copenhagen Consensus rated the fight against HIV/AIDS as the most important issue facing the world, and our State of the Future Index studies also show this as one of the most important threats to the future in quantitative terms. Another study showed that spending $60 billion to promote condom use and distribute antiretroviral drugs would save $3 trillion. Meanwhile, nurses and teachers in some parts of Africa are dying of AIDS faster than they can be replaced. Yet some important progress is being made: the yearly cost of antiretroviral medicine available to some in developing countries has fallen as low as $300 per person, a new 40-hour AIDS test may affect the spread of the disease, and a genetically modified vaginal bacteria that can be stored in freeze-dried tablets may be able to protect women against HIV.

While the number of major armed conflicts (those with 1,000 or more deaths) continues to fall, some major powers have not fully understood that Industrial Age military force is not sufficient to counter asymmetrical warfare. Engagement of the disenfranchised by the more powerful is essential to reducing terrorism and ethnic conflicts. This engagement will be increasingly important since, according to one study, there are 285 minority groups that could be in future conflicts due to different forms of injustice, and within the next 25 years it is possible that single individuals acting alone might use advances in science and technology to create and use weapons of mass destruction. There are more than 53,000 UN peacekeepers (military personnel and civilian police) from 96 countries currently deployed in 15 missions on three continents. Yet the vast majority of the world is living in peace, trans-cultural ethics is being studied, dialogues among differing worldviews are increasing, formal EU and informal East Asia regional groupings of powers are adding to stability, and intra-state conflicts are increasingly being settled by international interventions.

Next year marks the tenth anniversary of the Fourth World Conference of Women in Beijing—the largest UN conference in history. Although it accelerated efforts to improve women's lives, many nations have not fulfilled their commitments to international conventions, declarations, and platforms for improving the status of women in their countries, even though this could be one of the most cost-effective strategies for addressing the global challenges of our age. Meanwhile, violence against females between 15 and 44 years of age causes more death and disability than cancer, malaria, traffic accidents, and even war. Amnesty International estimates that one out of every three women has been physically assaulted by an intimate male partner at some point in her life.

The more than $2 trillion amassed per year by transnational organized crime allows its participants to buy the knowledge and technology to create new forms of crime to generate even more profits. Nation-states can be understood as a series of decision points that are vulnerable to the vast amounts of money from crime syndicates. Transnational organized crime is increasingly interfering with the ability of governments to act. It is time for an international campaign by all sectors of society to develop a global consensus for action to counter transnational organized crime.

Most people do not appreciate how fast science and technology will change over the next 25 years. People are surprised to learn that even today we can see proteins embedded in a cell's membrane tens of billionths of a meter across, that organic transistors with a single-molecule channel length have been developed, that gene variants for schizophrenia, depression, and other mental diseases have been discovered, and that light has been stopped by a yttrium-silica crystal and then released and has been slowed in gas and then accelerated, promising vast improvements in computer capacity. The synergies and confluence of nanotechnology, biotechnology, information technology, and cognitive science—known as NBIC—will dramatically increase individual and group performance and the support systems of civilization. Dramatic increases in collective human-machine intelligence are possible within 25 years.

Today, it takes 33% less energy to produce a unit of GDP in industrial economies than it did in 1973. Nevertheless, world energy demand is forecast to increase by 54% from 2001 to 2025 and to require about $16 trillion in new investments to meet demands by 2030. A Millennium Project international panel rated the commercial availability of non-nuclear fission and non-fossil fuel means of generating baseload electricity by 2025 at prices competitive with today's fossil fuels as the most important mission for science and engineering to improve the future. Unless significant progress is made on carbon sequestration, the environmental movement may try to close down the fossil fuel industries, just as it stopped atomic energy growth 30 years ago.

The synergies of NBIC technologies plus robotics and genomics promise god-like powers with ethical implications beyond current discourse. Information overload makes it increasingly difficult to separate the noise from the signal of what is important to know in order to make a good decision. Because the unprecedented speed of change makes people unsure about the future and because globalization is challenging philosophical and religious certainty, people are unsure of the basis on which to make decisions. Chapter 1 presents executive summaries of 15 Global Challenges for humanity, while more substantial details for each are included in the CD's Chapter 1.

State of the Future Index

On what basis should the world's resources be allocated on behalf of humanity? The State of the Future Index is a tool in development to help answer that question. It is a statistical combination of key indicators and forecasts related to 15 Global Challenges as a whole that assesses whether the future is improving or getting worse over the next 10 years. It integrates expert judgments from around the world to answer in quantitative terms which issues deserve attention to diminish risk or improve the future.

Several years ago the Millennium Project examined the interaction among the Challenges and found that improving one improved most of the others, while deterioration in one makes the condition of all the Challenges worse. This led to the belief that more may be learned about effective policies by studying the relationships among the elements of a system than by studying the elements themselves. Why not search for the policies that have the most beneficial effects across the set of issues? SOFI provides a mechanism for doing just that. With SOFI, someone could conceive a hypothetical policy and test it to determine not only whether it promises to satisfy its primary intent but what its overall effect will be on the general future outlook.

This year, new software was developed to ease the chore of data entry and the computation of the SOFI. Sensitivity tests were performed to determine the response of the SOFI to changes in assumptions about two or three key external developments. The policies that held the key to the future were found to be associated with lowering the projected number of AIDS deaths and diminishing the probability of a high number of deaths due to terrorism. Without effective policies in these areas, there is a significant chance of a much darker future, with a SOFI sharply lower than it might have been. (See Figure 1 for a graphic representation of the 2004 SOFI.)

The future cannot be reduced to a number, but the process of developing this index forces people to consider what they mean when they say the future is getting better or worse. An international panel of more than 200 scientists, business planners, decisionmakers, and futurists who work for international organizations, governments, corporations, NGOs, and universities identified and rated developments that might alter the SOFI variables. Chapter 3 presents an executive summary of these insights, and the full details can be found in the CD's Chapter 2. Chapter 4 introduces the first national SOFIs.

2004 State of the Future Index Figure 1

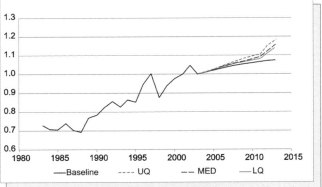

Middle East Peace Scenarios

The time and energy it would require to rectify past injustices felt today might be better spent on building a more just, humane future. We do not have to forget the past, but we should not let it enslave our ability to build a better tomorrow together. In this spirit, at the suggestion of the Cairo Node of the Project, the Millennium Project agreed to produce three alternative normative peace scenarios for the Israeli-Palestinian situation. Even though this conflict is one of the most analyzed issues today, there are no well-researched, objective, plausible peace scenarios for the Middle East—not frameworks, proposals, treaties, or road maps, but scenarios that are stories with causal links connecting the future and the present.

Working backward from an imagined peace sometime in the future, seven conditions were identified that had to exist just before peace was achieved. Actions to address each precondition were identified and rated by an international panel as to their likelihood, the importance of achieving the precondition, and the possibility that it could backfire or make things worse. The results from a two-round questionnaire were used to write draft scenarios, which were submitted to the panel members for comment. The pattern of results of this third round was used to write the three scenarios presented in Chapter 5. These can now be used as a basis for discussion among the interested parties. The full study with the results of all three rounds is available on the CD.

Scenario 1: Water Works—Water crises led to water negotiations that built trust that peace was possible and boosted political negotiations. Momentum increased with new youth political movements, the "Salaam-Shalom" TV series complemented by Internet peace phone swarms, tele-education in refugee camps, the Geneva Accords complemented by parallel hardliner negotiations, joint development with Arab oil money and Israeli technology, participatory development processes, new oil pipelines from the Gulf to the Mediterranean, and a unique "calendar-location matrix" for time-sharing of the holy sites. UN troops enforced agreements with non-lethal weapons, and new forms of international collaboration cemented the peace.

Scenario 2: The Open City—The new Pope challenged Jewish and Muslim religious leaders to solve the question of governance in Jerusalem. Politics, power, and media all played a role in reaching a proposed solution that was ultimately codified in a resolution adopted by the UN General Assembly. The threat of a fatwa ended the suicide bombings; when the bombings stopped, so did the Israeli retaliatory missions. Education of young Muslims gradually changed; schools that once taught hatred moderated. On the question of refugees, the Israelis were concerned about being overwhelmed and outvoted by Palestinian immigrants in their democratic society. The issue promised to be inimical but a compromise restricted the right to vote to people who had lived in Israel for more than seven years. Finally, a historic proposal came to the UN from Israel—it traded guarantees of Israeli security for establishment of a permanent Palestinian state.

Scenario 3: Dove—"Dove" was a secret, contested Israeli plan to de-escalate and unilaterally renounce retaliation in order to demonstrate that Palestinians were aggressors. At the same time, a secret debate was taking place among extremist Palestinians on whether to escalate to more lethal weapons. Those against escalation said "If we desist, Israel will be seen as the aggressor." So each side had reasons for wanting to stop but seemed frozen by circumstances. The tide changed when 27 Israeli pilots said they would not participate in future air raids, initiating the "Refusnik" movement. What happened next was like a chess game. The Israelis got a guarantee that the bombing would stop; the Palestinians got an agreement that the Israelis would withdraw to the pre-1967 borders. A series of non-aggression treaties and agreements stated that Israel had a right to exist. Jerusalem became an open city, with its own democratic government. Immigration quotas were established. Foreign capital flowed into the area. New businesses were established, and unemployment among the Palestinians dropped sharply. It was a self-fulfilling cycle: the move toward peace sparked the environment for peace.

While writing these scenarios, it became increasingly clear that the speed of building better conditions must be so fast that the voices of those who would have us understand the past before we move forward are less audible than before. It is a race. It is easy to say there are many alternative scenarios for the Middle East that show variations on the current violence, but without plausible stories of how peace could evolve with cause-and-effect relations woven into peace scenarios, it is difficult to motivate people to move toward more cooperative pursuits to build a new story for the region.

Environmental Security

The links between the environment and security are increasingly becoming the subject for international agreements. Environmental security is environmental viability for life support with three sub-elements: preventing or repairing military damage to the environment, preventing or responding to environmentally caused conflicts, and protecting the environment due to the moral value of the environment itself. The Millennium Project has been scanning a variety of sources to identify emerging environmental issues with treaty and military implications. Over 200 items have been identified during the last two years. A summary is presented in Chapter 6, and the full text of these items and their sources can be found in CD Chapter 9.1, Emerging Environmental Security Issues. Some general patterns and insights from the items include:

- "Business as Usual" will be a misleading forecast: New sensor technologies, increasing environmental awareness, and international agreements mean that many actions accepted over the past 10–20 years will not be tolerated over the next decade or two.

- Military roles are increasing in documenting military chemicals, food, equipment, and impacts and locations of weapons (such as the spent uranium shelling controversy), in securing pathogens and toxins from terrorists, in conducting more-sophisticated post-conflict clean ups, and in anticipating disaster responses as the impact and number of disasters rises and as disasters become more acute due to climate change and chemical and biological pollution.

- Environmental causes of conflicts are expected to become more significant as environmental deterioration increases the number of "environmental refugees," which will in turn increase the number and scale of conflicts related to migration.

- Environmental issues continue to rise on the international political agenda.

- The Aarhus Convention reinforces the growing trend of increased public and NGO participation in shaping national, regional, and international policy, legislation, and treaties.

- Sovereignty and environmental security may increasingly be in conflict.

- Global warming is not going away, and legal mechanisms to recover damage seem inevitable.

- A global framework for chemical, nuclear, and biological weapons is needed.

- New initiatives to increase eco-efficiency and eco-security are emerging all over the world and at all levels—the UN, regional groups, and national and local organizations.

Weblog Database

There are many methods for exploring prospects for the future, but probably the most fundamental way to support futures research is using a system to identify developments that promise change and to keep track of changes that are under way. Such a system is referred to as an early warning or environmental scanning system. The term "environmental" in this case does not refer to nature but to the "environment" being scanned for change. This could be the social, political, technological, or economic as well as the natural environment.

To facilitate an evolving collective intelligence, the Millennium Project is creating a weblog database to monitor global change and to update and improve the 15 Global Challenges and the State of the Future Index (see Chapter 7). Comments on the entries can be made by anyone (with editorial oversight). From time to time the entries will be reviewed for possible input to the 15 Global Challenges and SOFI. The results will be placed into a knowledge database tailored to support the updating process. This will provide an additional on-going feedback system to increase the collective intelligence of the Millennium Project. The database is available via a link at www.stateofthefuture.org.

Reinforcement for Previous Research

This year's research supports much of the Project's previous research, which merits repeating.

Globalization and advanced technology allow fewer people to do more damage, in less time, than ever before; hence, the welfare of anyone should be the concern of everyone. Such platitudes are not new, but the consequences of their failure will be quite different in the future than in the past.

Long-range goals like landing on the moon or eradicating smallpox that were considered impossible did excite many people who went beyond selfish, short-term interests to great achievements. The de facto decision system of the world is not adequately addressing the Global Challenges. The 15 Global Challenges or the eight UN Millennium Development Goals could be the basis for "trans-institutions"—a new concept of an institution that is composed of some income and personnel from governments, corporations, NGOs, universities, and international organizations without the majority from any one category of institution. Such trans-institutions would commit the resources and talent to address the goal and would act through each category of conventional institution.

Most people in the world may be connected to the Internet within 15 years, making cyberspace an unprecedented medium for civilization. This new distribution of the means of production in the knowledge economy is cutting through old hierarchical controls in politics, economics, and finance. It is becoming a self-organizing mechanism that could lead to dramatic increases in humanity's ability to invent its future.

Because weapons of mass destruction may be available to single individuals over the next generation, we should begin to explore how to connect education and security systems in a healthy way to prevent their use.

The cost of military operations to comply with environmental regulations may become so high that the nature of conflict and military operations could change.

There are many answers to many problems, but there is so much extraneous information that it is difficult to identify and concentrate on what is truly relevant. Since healthy democracies need relevant information, and since democracy is becoming more global, the public will need globally relevant information to sustain this trend.

The great paradox of our age is that while more and more people enjoy the benefits of technological and economic growth, growing numbers of people are poor and unhealthy and lack access to education. World leaders are increasingly seeking a common platform among UN organizations, the World Bank, the IMF, the WTO, multinational corporations, and other key actors of globalization in order to address this issue.

Creating global partnerships between the rich and poor to make the world work for all, which seemed like an idealistic slogan before September 11th, may prove to be the most pragmatic direction as the possibilities increase that individuals may one day have access to weapons of mass destruction.

The factors that caused the acceleration of S&T innovation are themselves accelerating; hence the acceleration of scientific and technological accomplishments over the past 25 years will appear slow compared with the rate of change in the next 25. The process of scientific R&D that uses peer-reviewed journals and government support is being challenged by those using venture capital and press releases to get products to the market more quickly. Since technology is growing so rapidly along several fronts, the possibility of it growing beyond human control must now be taken seriously. National decisionmakers have not been trained in the theory and practice of decisionmaking, and few know how advanced decision support software could help them. Formalized training for decisionmakers could result in a significant improvement in the quality of global decisions. In addition to policymakers needing training in how to make decisions, processes to set priorities (local, national, and international) need further development.

We know the world is increasingly complex and that the most serious challenges are global in nature, yet we don't seem to know how to improve and deploy Internet-based management tools and concepts fast enough to get on top of the situation.

The role of the state is more important in countries where there is little private-sector activity; hence policies that make sense in western industrial countries that include leadership from the private sector are less applicable in poorer regions.

When the actions of one country threaten the security of many, when do the many have the right to invade the one? The extent of national sovereignty continues to be a key element in the analysis of environmental security, terrorism, climate change, the International Criminal Court, and management of future S&T risks.

Since education is one of the fundamental strategies to address most global challenges, it is important to identify the most effective educational materials, curricula, and distribution media for global education as well as institutional arrangements to accelerate learning.

The lack of ethical behavior and moral underpinnings has given rise to a new hunger for global ethics and the need to identify common ethical norms. Coupled with this is the extraordinary growth of global standards and those who seek to meet them through mechanisms such as the International Organization for Standardization.

Although many people criticize globalization's potential cultural impacts, it is increasingly clear that cultural change is necessary to address global challenges. The development of genuine democracy requires cultural change, preventing AIDS requires cultural change, sustainable development requires cultural change, ending violence against women requires cultural change, and ending ethnic violence requires cultural change. The tools of globalization, such as the Internet and global trade, should be used to help cultures adapt in a way that preserves their unique contributions to humanity while improving the human condition.

The 15 Global Challenges Identified and Discussed

1. How can sustainable development be achieved for all?

2. How can everyone have sufficient clean water without conflict?

3. How can population growth and resources be brought into balance?

4. How can genuine democracy emerge from authoritarian regimes?

5. How can policymaking be made more sensitive to global long-term perspectives?

6. How can the global convergence of information and communications technologies work for everyone?

7. How can ethical market economies be encouraged to help reduce the gap between rich and poor?

8. How can the threat of new and reemerging diseases and immune microorganisms be reduced?

9. How can the capacity to decide be improved as the nature of work and institutions change?

10. How can shared values and new security strategies reduce ethnic conflicts, terrorism, and the use of weapons of mass destruction?

11. How can the changing status of women help improve the human condition?

12. How can transnational organized crime networks be stopped from becoming more powerful and sophisticated global enterprises?

13. How can growing energy demands be met safely and efficiently?

14. How can scientific and technological breakthroughs be accelerated to improve the human condition?

15. How can ethical considerations become more routinely incorporated into global decisions?

1.

GLOBAL CHALLENGES

Chapter 1 presents two-page descriptions of 15 Global Challenges that have been identified and updated through an ongoing Delphi process and environmental scanning since 1996. These Challenges are transnational in nature and transinstitutional in solution. They cannot be addressed by any government or institution acting alone. They require collaborative action among governments, international organizations, corporations, universities, NGOs, and creative individuals. Although listed in sequence, Challenge 1 on sustainable development is no more or less important that Challenge 15 on global ethics. The Challenges are interdependent: an improvement in one makes it easier to address others; deterioration in one makes it harder to address others. Arguing whether one is more important than another is like arguing that the human nervous system is more important than the respiratory system. There is greater consensus about the global situation as expressed in these Challenges and the actions to address them than is evident in the news media. The 15 Challenges provide a framework to assess the global and local prospects for humanity (sustainable development could be discussed as a global or a neighborhood objective).

More detailed treatments of the Global Challenges are available in the CD's Chapter 1, totaling nearly 600 pages. The international Delphi panels were selected by Millennium Project Nodes around the world for their knowledge and creativity as futurists, scholars, business planners, scientists, and decisionmakers who work for governments, private corporations, NGOs, universities, and international organizations. Both print and CD versions are the cumulative and distilled range of judgments from approximately 1,700 participants. See the Appendix for the demographics of the participants and see the CD's Appendix A for the full list of participants. Full details of the questionnaires and interview protocols that have been used from 1996 to 2004 to generate both the short and more detailed treatments of these Challenges are available at www.acunu.org/millennium/lookout.html.

Some of the Figures used to illustrate progress and prospects for the Challenges use the State of the Future Index calculations with trend impact analysis. Chapter 3 details this methodology.

The CD contains a more comprehensive overview of each Challenge, alternative views or additions to the overview, regional views and relevant information from recent literature, a set of actions from previous Global Lookout Panels with a range of views from interviews with decisionmakers augmented by new items and views over the past year, additional actions and views on those actions, and suggested indicators to measure progress or lack thereof on each Challenge.

1. How can sustainable development be achieved for all?

Wildfires annually burn an area half the size of Australia and generate nearly 40% of total CO_2 emissions. The cumulative volume of greenhouse gases produced by fossil fuel consumption over the next 50 years could more than double the output during the last 50 years. The Intergovernmental Panel on Climate Change estimates a 1.4–5.8 degrees Celsius warming by century's end, which could raise sea levels by 34 inches, changing human coastal settlements and melting the polar ice cap. Already, atmospheric CO_2—which for 400,000 years fluctuated between 180 and 280 ppm—has reached 380 ppm. Only human activity can explain this change, says the US National Academy of Sciences. Three of the last five years were the hottest in recorded history, glaciers are receding worldwide, and global temperature changes threaten entire ecosystems, causing some species migration and having new consequences for human health. Climate change may threaten more than 1 million species with extinction by 2050. The legal foundations are being laid to sue for damages caused by greenhouse gases.

Humanity may have consumed more natural resources since World War II than in all of history prior to that time. Half the world's forests and 25% of the coral reefs are gone. Some 9.4 million hectares of forest area are lost annually worldwide. World leaders' declarations on sustainable development have not yet been matched by concerted actions for global change. The April 2004 meeting of the UN Commission on Sustainable Development reinforced the need for strategic investments in water, sanitation, and human settlements to meet the commitments of the WSSD. The synergy between economic growth and technological innovation has been the most significant engine of change for the last 200 years, but unless we improve our economic, environmental, and social behavior, the next 200 years could be difficult.

Next to the proliferation of weapons of mass destruction, unsustainable growth may well be the greatest threat to the future of humanity. Yet without sustainable growth, billions of people will be condemned to poverty, and much of civilization will collapse.

The public has to be engaged through massive educational efforts via television, music, games, movies, and contests that stress the quality of human beings in harmony with nature along with what individuals and groups can do to change consumer behavior, initiate environmental tax reforms, and move from a fossil fuel economy toward a knowledge-consciousness economy. We should bring scientists and engineers from around the world together with new leadership from UN Global Compact corporations to stimulate investments into more-sustainable solutions; establish an environmental crimes international intelligence and police unit; create definitions and measurements for commonly applied tax incentives and labels for more environmentally friendly products; abolish environmentally inefficient subsidies; include environmental costs in the pricing of natural resources and products; invest in socially responsible businesses; spread the environmental standards ISO 14000 and 14001 to more countries and companies; create an international public/private funding mechanism for high-impact technologies such as carbon sequestration or space solar power and for acquiring the rights to innovate "green" technologies; declare key habitats off-limits for human development; consider the establishment of a World Environment Organization with powers like the WTO; encourage synergy between environmental movements and human rights groups to make clean air, water, and land a human right; and demonstrate how to change complacency and consumption while increasing efficiency and improving living standards.

Regional Perspectives

AFRICA: Tie local self-help to government budgets, coordinate natural resources management planning and training continent-wide, combat AIDS as a top priority, and create partnerships between internal development organizations and international funding and technical assistance agencies. Continued stability and economic growth in South Africa, Nigeria, and Egypt could provide the basis for the continent's long-term development.

ASIA AND OCEANIA: Most of the 2 billion people vulnerable to increases in floods due to climate change and population growth by 2050 will be in Asia. Rapid urbanization and economic growth over the next generation will require massive efforts to supply additional electricity. China and then India will eventually emit more greenhouse gases than the United States. China has no choice but to create new approaches to sustainable development. China has to feed over 22% of the world's population with less than 7% of the world's arable land. Japan is a world leader in environmentally friendly cars, but still it is not likely to meet its Kyoto target due to the recent shutdown of its nuclear power stations and increasing emissions. India loses over 10% of its GDP per annum because of loss in agricultural productivity, health costs due to polluted air and water, and costs due to depleted water resources.

EUROPE: The EU as a whole is not expected to make the Kyoto targets for lowered greenhouse gases emissions by 2010; with existing policies, only the United Kingdom, Sweden, and seven new EU members are expected to reach their targets. The EU also expects to begin trading in greenhouse gas emissions in 2005. Ethnic conflict and growing crime get in the way of Central and East European efforts toward sustainability. Because feedback mechanisms are not well established in Central and Eastern Europe, there is little trust in a free system, and consequently apathy spreads.

LATIN AMERICA: Guerrillas, paramilitaries, and drug dealers create political instability, displacing farmers and leading to irrational uses of the land. Brazil is the world's leading biodiversity hotspot and rainforest conservation site. Attacks on land tenure and the breakup of farms into smaller parcels is generating irreversible ecological damage in most countries. Decentralize the decisionmaking process, move from sectoral to integrated development approaches funded by international agencies, and stop deforestation.

NORTH AMERICA: Without serious change, total US greenhouse gas emissions will increase 43% between 2000 and 2020, raising temperatures in the 48 contiguous states by 3-5 degrees Celsius this century. Agricultural and energy subsidies should be eliminated and research should be done to convert CO_2 emissions into useful by-products such as sugars, proteins, and starches. Within the next 10 years we could develop nanobiological solutions to our toxic agricultural practices. As the world's largest consumer, largest producer of greenhouse gases, and largest economic power and as a role model for the developing world, North America has to make major changes: resolve the conflict between corporations' short-term profits and long-term sustainability, eliminate corporate subsidies, invest in socially responsible businesses, publish indicators of progress, and demonstrate how to reduce consumption while increasing efficiency and improving living standards.

Figure 2

World Mean Monthly Carbon Dioxide in Atmosphere

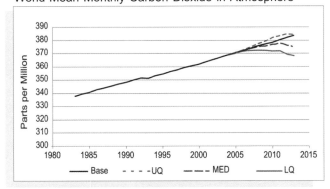

Source: NOAA Climate Monitoring and Diagnostics Laboratory, US Department of Commerce, with Millennium Project estimates

2. How can everyone have sufficient clean water without conflict?

Without major changes, by 2050 more than 2 billion people will be in water-scarce areas according to the *World Water Report* of 23 UN agencies. Today, water tables are falling on every continent, agricultural land is becoming brackish, groundwater aquifers are being polluted, 1.1 billion people do not have access to safe drinking water, and 2.4 billion people lack adequate sanitation. About 80% of all diseases in the developing world are water-related; many are related to poor management of human excreta. Urbanization is increasing water demands faster than many systems can supply, which increases the potential for rich-poor and urban-rural conflicts. Agriculture accounts for 70% of all human usage of fresh water, and according to FAO, water for agriculture needs to increase 60% to feed an additional 2 billion people by 2030. About 40% of humanity lives in the 260 major international water basins shared by more than two countries; history shows that water-sharing agreements have occurred even among people in conflict and have led to cooperation in other areas.

Increased demand for water also poses severe threats to the ecosystem. More than 3,000 fresh-water species are listed as threatened, endangered, or extinct, and the degrading ecosystem will undermine human welfare in the long run. Achieving the UN Millennium Development Goal of halving the number of people without safe drinking water by 2015 will require 342,000 more water connections and 460,000 sanitation connections every day from now until 2015. The World Panel on Financing Water Infrastructure estimated that the $80 billion spent annually on water systems for developing and transition nations will have to reach $180 billion in 20–25 years to meet humane water standards.

More empirical studies are needed to resolve the mixed reviews of privatization strategies for water supply. We have to produce more food with less water. Use the UN's 2005–15 Decade: Water for Life, the UN MDG goal on water, and the World Water Assessment Programme to focus knowledge and political will on addressing this challenge, and create an international water organization to finance and focus research on increasing water supply. Focus on changing agricultural practices to get more crop per drop of water: better manage rain-fed irrigation, selectively introduce water pricing, add drip irrigation and precision agriculture, invest in watershed management, integrate water management plans, and develop plants that are drought-hearty and more brackish-tolerant. Convert degraded farmlands to forest or grasslands. Water scarcity will be solved by increased energy to transport, desalinate, and improve water distribution. Other investments should go to household sanitation, wastewater treatment, reforestation, water storage, and treatment of industrial effluents in multipurpose water schemes. Construct eco-friendly dams, pipelines, and aqueducts to move water from areas of abundance to areas of scarcity. Water can also be conserved by using animal stem cells to produce meat tissue (without the need to create the animal) and by increasing vegetarianism around the world. Replicate successful community-scale projects around the world. Finally, countries need to continually update national and regional water plans.

Regional Perspectives

AFRICA: About 38% of Africans do not have access to safe water and sanitation. One-third of Africa's fresh water flows through just one river, the Congo, while only about 10% of Africa's population lives within the Congo's drainage basin. Economic development of Sudan and Ethiopia will draw on the Nile, making water conflicts in this region seem inevitable without successful efforts such as the Africa Water Facility.

ASIA AND OCEANIA: One in three Asians lacks access to safe drinking water, and half the people living in the region do not have access to adequate sanitation. Forced migration due to water shortages has begun in China, and India should be next. In 10 years, even in the best-case scenario, the water situation in China will be worse and will not begin to improve for another 5–10 years. The average water resources per capita in China are only a quarter of the world average; some 400 cities face water shortage today, and the water supply situation in 100 cities is very serious. The International Water Management Institute estimates that aquifer depletion could reduce India's grain harvest by one-fourth. Asia's rivers have 20 times the recommended level of suspended solids, and the region is responsible for over 60% of the world's ocean-damaging, eco-system-destroying sediment flows. Polluted water causes more illness than people realize, increasing health costs and hindering development. Japan and UNDP have developed WaterShowcase, see <www.watershowcase.net>, to provide examples of best practices on this challenge.

EUROPE: Water scarcity is not a problem in Western Europe except in the south. Some water issues are managed through the EU. Water utilities in Germany pay farmers to switch to organic operations because it costs less than removing farm chemicals from water supplies. Current agricultural practice has to be improved to keep quality of both surface and groundwater. Much of the current water distribution infrastructure needs to be replaced. Land ownership is still not clear in many locations in the transitional economies, resulting in poor mining and timber management and affecting water quality, which was already polluted under previous administrations.

LATIN AMERICA: The $27-million Guarani Aquifer System Project will help Argentina, Brazil, Paraguay, and Uruguay implement a common framework for managing the 1.2 million-square-kilometer Guarani aquifer, South America's largest.

Approximately 85% of the region has basic water supply and 78% has sanitation, yet more than 130 million people still do not have safe drinking water in their homes. The laws are not effective and there is no culture of water efficiency. Megacities such as Mexico, Bogotá, São Paulo, and Buenos Aires will implode in 20 years if legal and financial actions are not implemented as planned. Moving people to middle-sized cities would provide a better quality of life and avoid conflicts. International and national treaties are beginning to have positive effects on water conflict trends in Mexico. Water purification is a problem in most urban systems. Biotechnology and applied sciences will provide a new approach to problem solving: food, health, and environment.

NORTH AMERICA: Although per capita water consumption has been lowered over 20 years, 16 million people face water rationing in the United States. Agricultural water subsidies under current government regulation encourage waste. Water could become a class problem; poor people will be the first victims in free market distribution. Drugs, hormones, and pesticides are beginning to show up in some water supplies, with unknown impacts.

Figure 3

Percentage of Households with Access to Safe Water
(15 most populated countries)

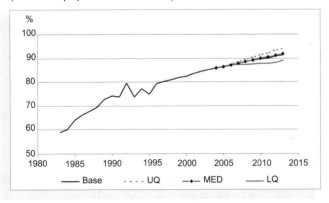

Source: WHO, Asia Recovery Data Information Center, World Development Indicators, with Millennium Project estimates

15

3. How can population growth and resources be brought into balance?

Assuming no major breakthroughs in life extension research, the UN forecasts that by the end of this century global population could be 5.5 billion (nearly a billion fewer than today), while the medium forecast is for 9.1 billion people in 2100. By 2050, if current trends continue, the fertility rates will fall below replacement for 75% of the world, the median age will increase from 26 today to 37, life expectancy will increase from today's 65 to 75, and there will be 2 billion people who are 60 or older—more people than are under the age of 15. Retirement and health care systems and culture will have to change. No industrial country has a fertility rate at or above the replacement level of 2.1 children per woman.

Although current population growth rates continue to slow and the food and energy efficiencies will increase, the sheer rising numbers of people mean it will be difficult to meet demands over the next 50 years. World grain harvest has fallen short of requirements four years in a row. The current population of 6.4 billion is forecast to grow to 8.9 billion by 2050; 98% of this growth is expected in poorer countries. The North is suffering from aging, declining populations and retirement benefits, while the South is suffering from growing populations having very limited opportunities. Almost 40% of the world lives in either China or India, where industrial growth is accelerating the use of resources and impacts on the environment. Nearly half the world lives in cities on 2% of the land, consuming about 75% of the resources and producing about the same percent of the pollution. Natural resources to support all this growth are shrinking. In 1997, a team of researchers estimated that nature's current value to the global economy is about $33 trillion a year and that 40% of the economy of the developing world is directly based on biodiversity, which is being destroyed.

More than 1 billion people live in slums and squatter communities, 25 countries are facing food emergencies, and about one out of every three children under five (150 million) is malnourished. Today's 3 billion city dwellers will grow to 5 billion by 2030. Without sufficient nutrition, shelter, water, and sanitation produced by more intelligent human-nature symbioses, increased migrations, conflicts, and disease seem inevitable. Once thought a problem, urbanization now seems part of the solution to poverty, ignorance, disease, and malnutrition.

To reduce the economic burden on the younger generations and keep up living standards, people will work longer and explore Internet-based businesses, other forms of tele-work, part-time work, and job rotation, as will retirement communities. The factors that reduced population growth in the developing world still need to be reinforced. These include increased income, improved literacy, diminished infant mortality, empowerment and education of women, urbanization, improved and inexpensive contraceptives, and family planning.

Lowered materials costs and better automation can cut inputs in half and double outputs; better ICT can more optimally match needs and resources worldwide in real time. FAO estimates that food production has to increase 60% over the next 20 years, irrigated land will have to increase by 22%, and water withdrawals by 14%. Better rain-fed agriculture and irrigation management, plus genetic engineering for higher-yielding, drought-tolerant crop varieties, will be needed. Currently, agriculture uses 80% of arable land in developing countries, of which 20% is irrigated. Without serious changes, 20% of developing countries will face water shortages within a generation, forcing mass migrations. The world demand for animal protein will accelerate as the middle class increases, triggering massive investments into genetically modified food, aquaculture, and stem cells for meat production.

Water and energy strategies for the growing population are discussed in Challenges 2 and 13.

Regional Perspectives

AFRICA: Millions of AIDS orphans could grow up in crime groups and join armed conflicts over natural resources, while much of the urban management class is being seriously reduced by AIDS. This pandemic has reduced life expectancy in Botswana from 67 in 1985 to 39 today; unless sexual practices change or medical breakthroughs occur, this will further decrease to 31 by 2015. Nevertheless, Africa's population is expected to grow from 13% of the world total in 2000 to 20% by 2050. In general, Africa is not managing its natural resources and has few plans to do so. Community-based natural resource management practices and security of land tenure are necessary to bring population and resources into balance.

ASIA AND OCEANIA: New technologies and people's ideas about procreation will change demographic forecasts. Asians earning more than $7,000 annually outnumber the total population of the United States, Canada, and Europe—laying the foundation for unprecedented consumption. With one-fifth of the world's total population, China has only 7% of the world's arable land. Mountains or deserts cover two-thirds of China, making the balance of the land available to 1.3 billion people. Under the UN medium scenario, India will be larger than China by 2050; 25% of Japan will be over 60 years old by 2015; and by 2080 Japan's population will be half of what it is today, forcing it to change its immigrant worker policies. Nearly 60% of all Arabs are under 25 years old and have poor prospects for employment.

EUROPE: Over 75% of the population increase in EU in 2003 came from cross-border migration. Increased immigrant labor to offset the aging and shrinking population will change European international relations, culture, and social fabric, which could lead to increasing social conflict.

LATIN AMERICA: Migratory policies should be adopted as an equilibrium factor for population distribution. Rapid urbanization is a major problem that is fed both by migration from rural areas and by high fertility among new arrivals in urban settings. There is a certain Malthusian cynicism about the solution to population and resource problems. The huge income gap drives political unrest, and 350–400 million people are hungry in the region.

NORTH AMERICA: The increasing Hispanic population in the United States could change American politics, culture, society, and trans-Atlantic relations in the long run. Biotech and nanotech are just beginning to make an impact on medicine; hence dramatic breakthroughs in longevity are inevitable in 25–50 years. New living areas on Earth, on oceans, and in space will be developed. Nanotech efficiencies will use less input per function and make things last longer. Reducing "throw-away" consumption in favor of knowledge and experience could change the population-resource balance. Smart growth and a focus on intellectual rather than material resources may offset changing demographics.

Figure 4

Food Availability
Calories/Capita Low Income Countries

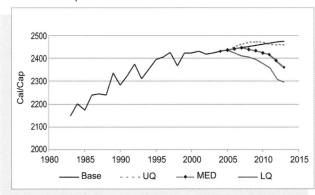

Source: FAO Foodstat Nutrition Database, with Millennium Project estimates

4. How can genuine democracy emerge from authoritarian regimes?

Although more people will vote this year than ever before in history, and although democracies are growing while dictatorships are decreasing, there are approximately 50 failed nation-states. Democracy is a mental attitude and a habit of behavior as well as responsible governance that protects group and individual rights and assures opportunity for meaningful participation in the political process. By conventional definitions, most people continue to live in democracies or partly free conditions rather than in dictatorships.

Although Freedom House says that "freedom and democracy continued to make overall progress worldwide in 2003 (25 countries demonstrated forward progress in freedom, while 13 registered setbacks)," the organization also found that press freedoms decreased last year (73 were rated free, 49 partly free, and 71 not free compared with 78, 47, and 68 respectively the previous year) and that the number of electoral democracies declined from 121 to 117. Nevertheless, democratization is a global long-term trend. Since democracies tend not to fight each other, and since humanitarian crises are far more likely to occur within authoritarian regimes, the trend toward democracy should lead to a more peaceful future.

Unfortunately, people can lose their incomes and social status during transitions to democracy. New democracies must address previous abuses of power to earn citizen loyalty, yet the pursuit of this justice can increase social discord and slow the process of reconciliation and democratic transition. Some recent democracies have not consolidated their democratic institutions and cultural changes; hence care has to be taken to prevent elected democracies from becoming tyrannies. To become genuine, young democracies emerging from authoritarian regimes need long-term economic stability, some experience with pluralism, and a majority of pro-democratic actors. Dramatic changes like multiparty elections, a free press, written constitutions, legal reforms,

and an independent judiciary do not automatically create a culture of democracy with citizen responsibilities.

The Internet has increased the opportunity for citizen feedback on public issues through e-government and other electronic means. As a result, governments are expected to become more accountable, transparent, and responsive to their citizens. Yet increasing sophistication and interaction among information technology, marketing, competitive intelligence, organized crime, and the potentials of information warfare raise the potential for the manipulation of information. Freedom of choice—inherent to democracy—implies judgment based on reliable information. Hence the development of methods to counter information manipulation will be important for continued democratization in the future. Democracy also needs strong rules against corruption and a smaller gap between rich and poor. Submission by the most powerful democracies to international law and transnational bodies is essential if democracy is to retain credibility in the eyes of people who have no direct experience with it.

Music, TV, movies, and education can nurture democratic cultures, as can policies for open communications, financial stability (reasonable credit access, stable currencies and exchange systems, security of assets, property ownership), and equitable judicial systems. Although making development assistance dependent on progress toward democracy has helped in some countries, a genuine democracy is achieved when the people—not an external organization—get the government to be accountable to them. Different areas may require different political systems at different times. However, all will be improved by increasing education, transparency, accountability, media access, initiatives that focus on corruption, and participation rather than waiting for others to solve problems. In addition, maintenance of "safety nets" and discussions among international political peers about successful transition strategies in the areas of the rule of law, respect for human rights, free media, tolerance of political opposition, free elections (visible UN Electoral Units where necessary), and an independent civil society all help develop the culture of democracy.

Regional Perspectives

AFRICA: Freedom House rated 11 countries in sub-Saharan Africa as free, 20 partly free, and 24 not free. Authoritarian regimes thrive on ethnicity and religious fundamentalism. Dictators in Africa will not yield their power until they have secure retirement situations. A proposed "African Council of Elders" could help if composed of former heads of state and initiated by someone like Nelson Mandela in association with the African Union to advise Africa, just like a village "council of elders." The Council could offer African leaders an attractive promotion and retirement from their governments. South Africa and Nigeria are the "linchpins" for Africa's political and economic progress.

ASIA AND OCEANIA: India is the world's largest democracy, with 600 million registered voters, and its 2004 national election is using electronic ballot machines. Asia is characterized by strong autocratic governments, which are only nominally democratic. With 1.3 billion people, China has a responsibility to provide stability during its political evolution. There is a growing gap between the information technology class and the illiterate. According to a recent Pew poll, 65% of Indonesians favor a democratic government compared with 32% who favor a strong leader. The Arab League approved the "Greater Middle East Initiative," which stresses democratic reforms.

EUROPE: With the addition of 10 countries to the EU, the revival of authoritarian regimes in Eastern and Central Europe is less likely, yet others argue it is a mistake to be dependent on the EU for

democratization. As people understand their potential, they will understand the importance of free decisions. There is a tension between Brussels bureaucracy and national democracy, and the intellectual tension between socialism and capitalism continues. Immigration-induced conflicts and policies may hinder democratization. Some see media restrictions in Russia and Kyrgyzstan as a sign that democracy may be receding.

LATIN AMERICA: A UNDP poll showed that a surprising number of Latin Americans were not sure that democracies give the best prospects for economic growth and security. Chile was a political dictatorship with economic freedom that made economic prosperity. Fewer than 50% of the citizens of this region vote. Now the challenge is for free-market democracies to include social justice, equity, and progress toward prosperity. If this is not achieved, then autocratic or totalitarian leaders will return with popular support. Cuba prohibits the use of the Internet in most homes.

NORTH AMERICA: Although the United States serves as a model to many, it is now corrupted by money, special interest lobbying, advertising, campaign contributions, and a "go-it-alone" foreign policy. Centralization of media and the Patriot Act have raised concerns about the future health of democracy in the United States. Democratic societies must continuously remember that democracy can be lost.

Figure 5

Percent of World Population Living in Countries That Are Not Free

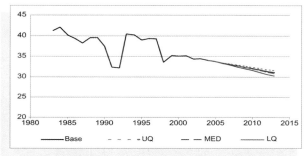

Source: Freedom House, US Census Bureau, with Millennium Project estimates

5. How can policymaking be made more sensitive to global long-term perspectives?

There is no escaping the need to educate the public, who could in turn elect more global future–minded politicians. International responses to SARS, the September 11th attacks, and Iraq have increased global thinking, but their impacts seem short-lived and have not had the same impact on long-term thinking. Yet the completion of the Human Genome Project, management of the International Space Station, globalization of the news media and Internet, and the evolution of the WTO, NATO, and the EU—all relatively unthinkable just 25 years ago—are some of the factors that demonstrate acceleration, complexity, and globalization, which increase the need for global, long-term perspectives. Globalization increases our awareness that we are all part of the "great chain of being," which will increase our compassion and global long-term thinking.

Unfortunately, the daily complexities of politics and the need to manage current problems still leave little time to consider the bigger picture. Narrow, short-term thinking is reinforced in all sectors of society. Corporate stockholders want quick profits, forcing corporate leaders to focus on actions that can improve the next quarter's profits; government leaders give priority to immediate issues to keep in power; NGO leaders who may look at the longer term often tend to do so only from the perspective of a single issue; leaders of international organizations also tend to focus on one issue and can be overwhelmed by the difficulty of addressing multiple issues on a global basis; and news executives are driven by daily deadlines and the need to keep people's attention by emphasizing the drama of the moment. As a result, decisionmakers feel little pressure to consider global long-term perspectives. Nevertheless, long-range goals like landing on the moon or eradicating smallpox that were considered impossible did excite many people who went beyond selfish, short-term interests to

great achievements. An international assessment of such goals is found in the CD's Chapter 7.

Countries should establish standing parliamentary "Committees for the Future," as Finland has done, and governments should establish structured interactions among their departments with more coherent, high-level guidance and coordination, while providing executive information management systems and dashboard software the reinforces global long-range thinking. We need a global institution to coordinate global long-range strategic foresight. In addition to annual allocations, government budgets should have some 5–10 year allocations attached to rolling 5–10 year scenarios and strategies.

Each of the 15 Global Challenges in this chapter and the eight UN Millennium Development Goals could be the basis for a different transinstitutional or international coalition composed of the governments, corporations, NGOs, universities, and international organizations that are willing to commit the resources and talent to address a specific goal. Since the annual calculation of the global State of the Future Index in Chapter 3 is based on indicators that relate to progress on global challenges, a 10-year forecast could imply that decisionmaking is increasingly taking global long-term perspectives into account. If national SOFIs were constructed and used in policymaking, then in order to make the index rise decisionmakers would have to pursue policies that address the longer term. Incentives need to be created to use SOFI, such as a criteria in World Bank loans or as the basis international awards to recognize the best efforts for global long-term decisionmaking. Maybe politicians' pensions should be dependent on their nation's GDP or SOFI.

We also need to create participatory processes informed by futures research, increase training and education courses in futures thinking, convert futures research methods into teaching methods to future-orient instruction, and organize data for easier use in foresight and policy analysis. Decisionmakers should be trained in futures research methods and required to communicate the longer-term implications of their decisions. This could lead to the use of futures methods in all forms of policymaking to develop, communicate, and revise future visions interactively among all sectors of society.

As the world becomes too complex to manage by nation-state hierarchies alone, new systems will emerge to better manage global long-term decisionmaking. National and international awards and recognition could be given to highlight global long-term consistent achievements (e.g., Nobel Peace Prize, MacArthur Fellowship, UN medals, and specific country awards). In addition to educating government, NGO, and corporate leaders, it is essential to empower and train local leaders and to encourage the movement toward identifying local issues with international counterparts.

Regional Perspectives

AFRICA: Nigeria announced plans to have most government services available online by 2008. Although UNDP/African Futures produced Africa 2025 scenarios that have contributed to long-range thinking among governments, the project was closed last year; its mission was to work with African governments to incorporate long-term perspectives into their mid- and short-term planning. Since the early 1980s, when some African countries had to launch structural adjustment programs, the issue of orienting policymaking toward a global long-term perspective has continually been raised.

ASIA AND OCEANIA: China is just beginning to emerge as a global long-range decisionmaker in the international arena. There is a tendency for Japanese people to think Japan is so different that they have difficulty thinking about global issues,

but Japanese corporations and the Keidanren are famous for long-term planning. South Korea is a world leader in broadband penetration due it its global long-range planning.

EUROPE: The debate about the contents of EU's constitution is also a debate about long-term perspectives. International diplomats and negotiators struggle each day to reach agreements that reflect long-term and global thinking. New ideologies are likely to evolve as a result of criticism of uncurbed capitalism and various forms of authoritarian regimes. European implications of aging populations for public finances and health systems, restructuring of energy systems, transport problems, sustainable development issues, and major geopolitical shifts such as the emergence of China are forcing global long-term thinking. The EU has increased funding for futures research.

LATIN AMERICA: UN conferences on global issues and education exchange programs help sensitize government officials. Recent and pending political changes in the region may force longer-range thinking. A new generation of leaders is emerging, which is opening the door to more long-term global perspectives.

NORTH AMERICA: As a technologically dynamic society, the United States bears a special responsibility for systems analysis, futures research, and technological forecasting and assessment. To improve acceptance of the long-term perspective, it would be useful to develop a collection of high impact cases in which foresight led to demonstrable benefits or lack of futures thinking proved costly. (See the CD's Chapter 10 for an initial study on this suggestion.) Recognition of future-oriented studies as a responsible scholarly field of study and inclusion of its study in educational curricula should eventually translate into decisionmaking that takes global long-term perspectives into account.

6. How can the global convergence of information and communications technologies work for everyone?

As the integration of cell phones, video, and the Internet grows, prices will fall, accelerating globalization and allowing swarms of people to quickly form and disband, coordinate actions, and share information ranging from stock market tips to bold new ideas (*meme epidemics*). China may pass the United States in the number of Internet users within two years; it already leads the world in cell phone users. Fifteen years ago few people had even heard of the Internet. Today it is the most powerful force in history for globalization, democratization, economic growth, and education, facilitating international management of everything from controlling the spread of SARS to accelerating scientific collaboration and creating new organizational forms that are changing the nature of governance. Fifteen years from now the majority of the world may be connected to the "planetary nervous system," making cyberspace an unprecedented medium for civilization. This new distribution of the means of production in the knowledge economy is cutting through old hierarchical controls in politics, economics, and finance. It is becoming a self-organizing mechanism for an emerging and collective computer/human intelligence, while international networks of experts are creating a more intelligent "Semantic Web" by defining concepts for common understanding among Internet users.

At the same time, civilization is vulnerable to cyber terrorism, power outages, information pollution (misinformation, pornography, junk e-mail, media violence), and virus attacks. (The probability of a catastrophic attack—global damages in excess of $100 billion from a chain of combined events—has risen from 2.5% for 2003 to about 30% for 2004, according to mi2g Ltd.) Microsoft says that these threats cannot be eliminated without a complete redesign of the PC, not expected before 2005–06. Junk mail at mid-2004 is expected to reach 80% of e-mails worldwide,

according to MessageLabs. Threats of information warfare, financial market vulnerability, fraud, loss of cultural diversity, terrorist intercommunications, and knowledge gaps all have to be addressed.

Meanwhile, millions will jump from no cameras right to cheap Internet cell phone cameras, with profound effects on global awareness. Mobile phones outnumbered fixed ones for the first time in 2002. Computer Industry Almanac estimates that in 2004 the Internet population will be close to 1 billion, and in 2007 might be 1.46 billion. In 1995, the United States had 75% of all Internet users in the world; today the digital divide is closing: there are 494.92 million Internet users in the industrial world and 290.79 million in the developing and transition worlds, for a ratio of 1 to 1.7. Even as a percent of penetration the gap is closing—from 41 to 1 in 1992 to 8 to 1 in 2002, according to ITU.

Forrester Research predicts that global e-commerce will expand to $6.9 trillion by 2004 and to $12.8 trillion by 2006. Sales on eBay increased 60% over a year to reach $24 billion in 2003. InfoTech Trends predicts that the global B2B market will reach $5.5 trillion in 2004. *The Economist* says "this market has the potential to become as perfect as it gets."

Even with low-cost Internet devices with direct satellite access and nonproprietary software freely available in public places, massive investments in educational software and multilanguage voice recognition and synthesis will be necessary to make these useful for the poor majority of the world. We should encourage global "collaboratories"; end national telecommunication monopolies; invent incentives to provide training for all; develop solar robot antennas that hover at high altitudes above the weather instead of a proliferation of microwave towers on land; use existing software to block offensive materials; use tele-

volunteers to help poorer regions; and redesign the PC to prevent viral damage.

Regional Perspectives

AFRICA: ITU estimates mobile telephone subscribers will reach 65 million by the end of 2005, up from an expected 59.7 million at the end of 2004. WiFi and WiMax will extend the reach of telecommunications into Africa. With AIDS devastating professionals, tele-education, tele-medicine, and e-government will be increasingly important. Africa is reported to have 12.25 million Internet users; since many share accounts and public access, however, the number might be considerably higher. Mobile phone connections overtook landline installations in Africa for the past five years; as Internet and mobile phones merge, African Internet usage should accelerate.

ASIA AND OCEANIA: Internet and B2B e-commerce grows fastest in this region, according to IDC. If trends continue, China will have 108 million Internet users by the end of 2004. The actual number in China is higher because of users in cyber cafes, schools, and multiuser accounts. The Gartner research group expects outsourcing revenue in India to increase by 65% during 2004, to $3 billion. Japan has the highest Multimedia Message Service adoption rate in the world. Over 80% of Japanese households and businesses are now online. South Korea has the world's highest broadband penetration. Madar Research estimates that by the end of 2005, Arab countries will have 25 million Internet users, which will be about 8% of the population.

EUROPE: Europe has 218 million Internet users. Forrester Research predicts the online retail market will take 8% of total retail sales by 2009. The Scandinavian region is the 2004 world leader in "e-readiness ranking" done by the Intelligence Unit of *The Economist*. Information control creates unprecedented, unthinkable challenges for democracy. The Internet is frag-

menting shared local beliefs but unifying beliefs globally. IDC forecasts that Linux usage will grow rapidly, accounting for almost a third of shipments in the Nordic countries within five years. The EU will create the European Network and Information Security Agency to counter Internet threats. IDC estimates that in Western Europe B2B e-commerce will increase at a compound annual growth rate of 91% from 2001 to 2005.

LATIN AMERICA: Joint partnerships made possible by the Internet are crucial for the region's development. Only a minority of people consider the Internet for cultural and educational purposes; most see it in terms of business and entertainment. Internet users in Latin America will reach 60.6 million by 2004, predicts eMarketer. Argentina, Brazil, and Mexico will account for 65% of these.

NORTH AMERICA: Internet2 connects 300 organizations at 10 gigabits per second. The United States and Canada have 228 million Internet users. US broadband users increased 42% over the previous year. The United States has more computers than the rest of the world combined. Latino Americans are the fastest-growing online ethnic group, while Asians are making more purchases via the Internet than any other ethnic group, according to The Media Audit.

Figure 6

Regional Internet Usage and Penetration
(population for 233 countries and regions of the world)

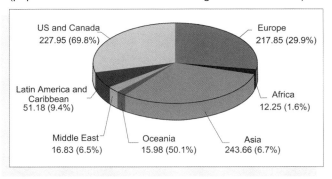

Source: Internet World Stats

7. How can ethical market economies be encouraged to help reduce the gap between rich and poor?

The ratio of the average income of people in the top 5% to the bottom 5% has grown from 6 to 1 in 1980 to over 200 to 1 now. Some 20% of the world receives 80% of the income. In addition to the moral implications, the disparity in wealth could lead to increased migration of the poor to richer regions, resulting in conflict. Although the world economy has grown to $33 trillion—with dramatic increases in life expectancy, primary school enrolments, access to safe drinking water and sanitation, and decreases in infant mortality—without major policy interventions the disparities could grow enough to create global instabilities. Agricultural subsidies in OECD countries that hurt developing countries' trade totaled $257 billion and provided 32% of OECD farmers' income.

Economic growth in India and China will be a major engine for meeting the UN MDG of halving world poverty by 2015, because 66% of the people living on just $1 a day are in Asia. Although significant growth has occurred in some developing countries, income per capita has been dropping steadily over the past 30 years in poorer areas, and remittances have become a major source of foreign currency. According to the World Bank, people living on less than $1 a day dropped from 40% to 21% of global population between 1981 and 2001, while the number of people living on $2 a day increased. GDP per capita in all developing countries rose by 30% during the same 20 years, but the rich-poor gap is getting wider within richer as well as poorer countries.

We need to create a flexible global strategic plan that uses the strength of free markets with rules based on global ethics. People in the top 5% of income should make special attempts to aid the bottom 5%, following the examples of Ted Turner, Bill Gates, and George Soros. International meetings have recommended improved international financial governance, increased trade, debt relief, national economic policy reforms, mobilization of domestic financial resources, reduction of corruption, and the creation of partnerships among development actors. The IMF now allows countries in arrears to negotiate new agreements, pending policy conditions.

Ethical market economies are encouraged when people have a "level playing field" guaranteed by an honest judicial system and by governments that provide political stability, a chance to participate in local development decisions, business incentives to comply with social and environmental goals, fairer trade, a healthy investment climate, and access to land, capital, and information. Since capital flows to profit potential, ethical activities have to be shown to be profitable and corporations have to be held accountable. Unfortunately, corruption and organized crime are still major impediments to development.

Richer nations should cut harmful agricultural subsidies, open their markets, and provide 0.7% of their GDP to aid poorer nations. We have to replace welfare attitudes with entrepreneurial spirit, reinforced by expanded microcredit mechanisms coupled with technical assistance, while using state welfare in states with little private sector. International taxes to internalize current externalities can generate extra funds to finance global public goods and global governance reforms.

Regional Perspectives

AFRICA: The number of people living on $1 a day doubled over the last 20 years in sub-Saharan Africa. Self-defeating attitudes among the poor should be replaced with entrepreneurial spirit. Africa is not likely to create ethical and dynamic markets until cultures become open to independent, critical thinking and produce favorable climates for foreign investment. Reorient the WTO toward meeting needs of developing countries. To reduce poverty by 50% in sub-Saharan Africa by 2015, national economies would have to average 7% growth a year—more than twice the current rate. The role of the state is more important where there is little private sector. Some question whether ethical markets can exist, since markets are driven by the profit motive and ethical entrepreneurship is not well known in Africa. Others point out that ethical markets can be created in the interests of the rich as well as the poor.

ASIA AND OCEANIA: East Asian GDP per capita has tripled since 1981; extreme poverty fell from 58 to 16%, and in China it fell from 64 to 17%. The majority of the poorest live in Asia. China averaged almost 9% annual growth in GDP per capita in the 1980s and 1990s and 7–8% recently. Vietnam saw growth of almost 6% in the 1990s, which reduced poverty by more than a third between 1993 and 1998, followed by 7% during 2000 and 2001. Economic initiatives that develop material civilization can be combined with those that develop spiritual civilization. Competition and symbiosis (encouraged by real socialism and some religions), along with self-reliance (encouraged by Confucianism and Taoism), are the bases of a more ethical market economy. Some question if market economies have ever been ethical, but agree that greater political and financial transparency and accountability will help. Japan's return to economic growth will help the region. The keys to economic growth in the Middle East are the resolution of the Israeli-Palestinian conflict, the rule of law, and small business development.

EUROPE: The EU enlargement forces new inter-European poverty reduction efforts. A new economic system with autonomous individuals based on new knowledge and an emerging global ethics is evitable. Ethical markets require democracy and freedom of cultural expression based on values that are globally valid and respected and that are enforced by political measures and informed consumer behavior. Europe needs to

harmonize differences in law and environmental tax reform, submit statements of ethics and values to shareholders, and deregulate obstacles to productive activity. Development policy should change the "poverty of spirit" as well as economic poverty.

LATIN AMERICA: The financial infrastructure to create and support equality does not exist in the region. The gap between rich and poor is the primary cause of social instability in Latin America. Distribution of the means of production and land tenure must change with the participation of lower-income people in all phases of development projects. Without an educated middle class and active civil society, policies to help the poor are not likely. However, it is encouraging to see that the region has seen primary school enrollment rise from 67% in 1990 to almost 90% today.

NORTH AMERICA: Ethical markets are created by prices that include social and environmental costs, socially responsible investing, fuller business disclosures, and a fairer tax code that taxes social externalities like pollution. It is simply impossible to make everyone equal, but equal opportunity is possible.

Figure 7

People Living on Less Than $2 Per Day
(million, without China)

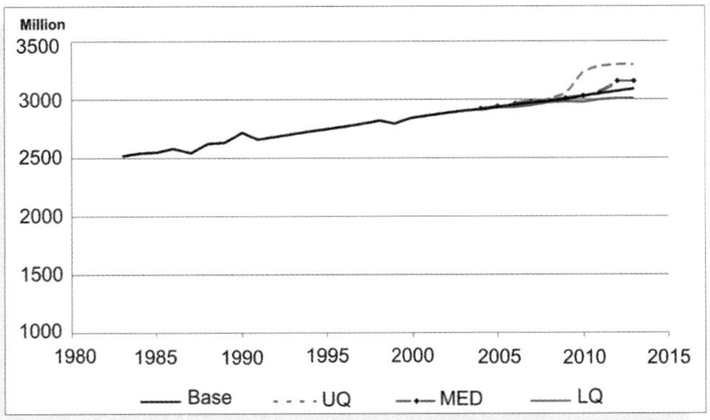

Source: World Bank Group, with Millennium Project estimates

8. How can the threat of new and reemerging diseases and immune microorganisms be reduced?

The Copenhagen Consensus rated the fight against HIV/AIDS as the most important issue facing the world. AIDS has killed 22 million people, while another 42 million are living with HIV/AIDS today. Although AIDS is the leading cause of death in sub-Saharan Africa, it is now spreading more rapidly in Eastern Europe and Central/Southern Asia. One study showed that spending $60 billion to promote condom use and distribute antiretroviral drugs would save the world $3 trillion. The yearly cost of antiretroviral medicine available to some in developing countries has fallen as low as $300 per person, and a new 40-hour AIDS test may affect the spread of the disease. Genetically modified vaginal bacteria may be able to protect women against HIV and to be stored in freeze-dried tablets. Meanwhile, bioterrorism is emerging as a threat on a par with nuclear war, triggering bio-sensor R&D for global deployment, general vaccines, and quarantine systems. The rapid and unprecedented international cooperation to contain SARS (which infected 8,000 people in 30 countries, killing more than 700) and avian flu (in process) is a key element in the emerging global system to address these threats. Human clinical trials for a SARS vaccine began a year after its outbreak.

Infectious diseases cause about 30% of deaths worldwide. More than 30 new and highly infectious diseases have been identified in the last 20 years, such as avian flu, Ebola, AIDS, SARS, and cross-species viruses in Africa; for many there is no treatment, cure, or vaccine. Furthermore, 20 known strains of diseases such as tuberculosis and malaria have developed resistance to antibiotics, while old diseases such as cholera, plague, dengue fever, meningitis, hemorrhagic fever, diphtheria, and yellow fever have reappeared. These developments are compounded by factors such as the rapid increase in international air travel and large populations who are malnourished and undereducated, living in unhealthy conditions. The globalization of trade, as well as recent changes in the production, handling, and processing of food and breeder stock, has heightened the risk of food-borne diseases. Activities such as deforestation, tourism, conflict, climate change, and migration into remote habitats have increased exposure to disease.

Incentives need to be created to change unhealthy behaviors that affect the world; one example is subsidies to help Hong Kong and Shanghai poultry farmers to replace their live-market businesses with frozen-products markets. The live markets in these cities are a key breeding ground for influenza. The responses to avian flu and SARS have shown that even without a vaccine it is possible to control a disease by preventing infection through early detection and accurate reporting, prompt isolation of those infected, and quarantine as needed.

Donors should increase their support for WHO's network of collaborating laboratories to improve the global surveillance system, strengthen the international rapid response system to infectious disease, and expand WHO's vaccines program. Additionally, support should be increased for applications of tele-medicine and tele-health; women's rights programs related to AIDS; safe water supply; advanced generations of antibiotics; innovative health measures such as the "Miracle Tree" (*Moringa*) in Senegal that is environmentally adaptable, edible as nutrition, and contains needed vitamins; and understanding the relationship among disease, ecology, and genetics. In the future, genetic engineering, stem cell research, and nanotechnology may one day be used to improve our immune systems to prevent infection by known and unknown viruses and disease; one vaccination could be permanent and heritable to future generations.

Regional Perspectives

AFRICA: Although prevalence of HIV/AIDS appears to remain stable, there is overall no decline in the epidemic. The high number of HIV infections can be lost in the total HIV/AIDS statistics by the equally high number of AIDS deaths. Only 75,000 people receive adequate AIDS medications in Africa; a WHO initiative would provide 3 million people with antiretrovirals by 2005. Some 14 million children have lost parents due to AIDS, a number that could grow to 42 million by 2010. Massive health education seems to have had little effect on changing African sexual behavior; some awareness programs are working, however: HIV prevalence was cut by one-third among young women in Addis Ababa from 1995 to 2001; Senegal's infection rate is 1.7%, while neighboring countries report rates of more than 10%. AIDS death rates among professionals are high enough to threaten development in many countries.

ASIA AND OCEANIA: SARS has improved regional health cooperation, which should affect other contagious diseases. By 2010, more people could have AIDS in Asia than in Africa. The 5 million in India with HIV/AIDS and 2 million in China show the early stages of the pandemic; UNAIDS forecasts 10 million in China will be infected by 2010. Malaria is endemic, outbreaks of dengue are common, and even in modern, sanitized Singapore there has been a resurgence of tuberculosis. With the massive influx of foreign workers, diseases that had almost disappeared are rapidly reemerging in South Korea.

EUROPE: Schools in Catalonia Spain are installing condom vending machines, defying the Catholic Church. Much of Russian and Central and East European health systems are near collapse, just as AIDS accelerates; Estonia has passed Russia in the prevalence of AIDS. Other problems in Europe come from migration and influenza. Future problems may come from synthetic bacteria from gene laboratories and unknown nano-organisms.

LATIN AMERICA: Although the region's traditional health indicators have improved, these are uneven among countries and population groups. Today communicable diseases (most of them curable) are responsible for about two-thirds of all deaths in Latin America and the Caribbean. However, 2 million people live with HIV/AIDS, which has helped tuberculosis to return to the region, and in many countries public health systems remain fragmented, bureaucratized, politicized, under-funded, and underreported in spite of widespread health sector reform efforts. Brazil is an exception with its success in reducing the growth of AIDS by massive public financing to produce nelfinavir domestically and give it free to its citizens.

NORTH AMERICA: Canada doubled its annual contribution to fight AIDS, tuberculosis, and malaria, while the United States pledged $15 billion over five years. Increased food imports raise vulnerability to infections from overseas. Society promotes the use and sale of antibiotics on scales that fuel growth of microbial resistance. New antibiotics and vaccines, rising living standards, responsible use of and leadership in biotechnology, and global and national systems of surveillance and response are critical to address health challenges. How can pharmaceutical companies be encouraged to invest in R&D for disease eradication that might not be too profitable but important to the poor majority?

Figure 8

Annual AIDS Deaths Worldwide

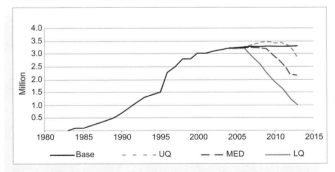

Source: Report on the Global HIV/AIDs Epidemic, UNAIDS, with Millennium Project estimates

9. How can the capacity to decide be improved as the nature of work and institutions change?

Information overload makes it increasingly difficult to separate the noise from the signal of what is important to know in order to make a good decision. Because the unprecedented speed of change makes people unsure about the future and because globalization is challenging philosophical and religious certainty, people are unsure of the basis on which to make decisions. The sheer number and intricacy of choices seems to be growing beyond our abilities to analyze and make decisions. Democratization and interactive media are adding to the number of people involved in decisionmaking, increasing complexity and making closure less likely than ongoing modifications of decisions. As decisionmaking to address global challenges becomes too complex, it will appear chaotic until new systems emerge. In the meantime, we know the world is increasingly complex and that the most serious challenges are global in nature, yet we don't seem to know how to improve and deploy appropriate management techniques or Internet-based management tools and concepts fast enough to get on top of the situation.

Since no government or other institution acting alone can address any of the global challenges in this chapter, transinstitutional decisionmaking has to be developed. Common platforms are needed that connect governments, corporations, NGOs, universities, and international organizations in collaborative decisionmaking. "The most creative agents of change may well be partnerships—among governments, private businesses, non-profit organizations, scholars and concerned citizens such as you," says UN Secretary-General Kofi Annan. Self-selection and self-organization of volunteers around the world via Web sites is a new strategy to increase transparency of public issues and to participate in decision processes. New participatory processes and other emergent transinstitutional systems using the Internet could

become informal decisionmaking systems that conventional powers ratify. Information pollution or "noise" in policy information could be reduced by software for knowledge visualization and mapping to help see a situation and various options at a glance.

The Internet is raising the pressure for all systems to be available worldwide 24 hours a day seven days a week. E-government systems are growing rapidly to help automate administrivia, make decisionmaking more transparent, and facilitate public participation, but they also create new vulnerabilities to manipulation by organized crime and to cyber-terrorism. UN organizations are the only trusted decisionmaking system for many people around the world. Yet these international organizations were designed for decisionmaking among governments, and have not synergistically evolved with private corporations, NGOs, and think tanks. There needs to be an emphasis on "partnership" between decisionmakers and decisiontakers and on the use of participatory processes. Foresight can play a significant role in decisionmaking processes, not just by deciding based on potential consequences but by drawing attention to the potential possibilities that can play out when decisions are made.

Many people believe it is possible to shape the future rather than simply prepare for a linear extrapolation of the present or a product of chance or fate. Just as efficiency is a key criterion in decisionmaking for industrial economies, wisdom will be a criterion in decisionmaking for successful knowledge economies.

We have to find ways for policymakers of all kinds to take decisionmaking training programs that might include e-government, decision-support software, risk taking and avoidance, advanced concepts in decisionmaking, prioritization processes, applications of cognitive science to decisionmaking, foresight, ways to work with new participatory processes, and collaborative decisionmaking with different institutions.

Regional Perspectives

AFRICA: The New Partnership for Africa's Development has begun operations to improve collaborative decisionmaking. The main problem in Africa is lack of good leadership and the ability to transfer power from one leader to the next. There is an African attitude toward power that the "winner-takes-all" of society's wealth and resources. Decisionmaking can be improved by developing civil society and NGO pressure for freedom of the press, accountability, and transparency of government; by adopting participatory decisionmaking practices and civil service reform; and by reversing the brain drain or connecting expatriates to the development processes back home through Internet systems.

ASIA AND OCEANIA: The drift of "ad-hocism" and "status-quoism" appears to be the regional systemic disease. Traditional hierarchical decisionmaking in Japan is beginning to be affected by NGOs. Regional dialogue and cooperation are needed to create a regional development plan. Special training for decisionmakers should be provided. Advanced information technology should be used for improved educational access, knowledge management, and decision support.

EUROPE: A list of firms with good decisionmaking should be organized. Europe is searching for its new identity, internally and in relation to the world as a whole. Improving decisionmaking is especially important now in the context of the enlargement of EU and NATO. Decisions can be improved through the use of scientific expertise, visionary leadership, decision tools like situation rooms, long-term perspectives, and the establishment of a global observatory. Advanced information technology may facilitate public participation in direct democracy. Transition economies need

public discussion of new development concepts, and more education and training for their leaders.

LATIN AMERICA: The region is increasingly demanding the modernization of state management and a new qualitative scale of state intervention. True leadership involves practice, education, and risk taking. It is a real pity that political leaders and candidates are not required to pass exams. Latin America has to improve political educational awareness and involvement of the people and to reduce corruption.

NORTH AMERICA: The Internet is a medium for self-organizing global brains that will become the de facto decisionmakers. The region will evolve using "subsidiarity," with decisions made at the lowest level appropriate to the problem. North Americans need to move from cause-effect, single-issue problem analysis to integrated, holistic visions and problem solving, using futures research, systems thinking, and technology assessment. Belief in easy, magical solutions seems to be growing, as problems are becoming less and less amenable to simple definitions or solutions. More courses in future-oriented studies should be established that stress relationships to decisionmaking. The media's simplistic treatments trivialize complex issues. There is a remarkable lack of training among politicians. Decisionmaking responsibility is being diffused through a complex workforce. People are increasingly working on many short-term jobs with changing "strategic partnerships." Many people are involved in volunteer activities and a diverse set of educational activities, some of them way beyond traditional retirement ages.

10. How can shared values and new security strategies reduce ethnic conflicts, terrorism, and the use of weapons of mass destruction?

Industrial-age military force is not sufficient to counter asymmetrical warfare. Engagement of the disenfranchised by the more powerful is essential to reducing terrorism and ethnic conflicts. Since chemical, biological, low-level nuclear ("dirty") bombs, and information warfare weapons of mass destruction and disruption may be available to individuals over the next 25 years, we have to learn how to connect education and security systems in a healthy way and to deal with a global environment in which the boundaries between war, civil unrest, terrorism, and crime are increasingly blurred. The clandestine transmission of nuclear capacities by a Pakistani scientist raised new concerns about proliferation. Since hospitals, food storage, water supply, and other support systems of civilization depend on the Internet, cyber weapons can now also be considered WMD.

The Stockholm International Peace Research Institute cites 19 major armed conflicts in 2003 that each had 1,000 or more deaths (down from 21 conflicts in 2002)—4 in Africa, 8 Asia, 3 the Americas, 3 Middle East, and 1 Europe (Afghanistan/Al Qaeda was classified as in the United States.) Ten of these conflicts were over the question of government and the remaining 9 over disputed territory. The vast majority of conflicts are intra-state, and civilian fatalities in these climbed from 5% in 1900 to more than 90% in the 1990s. Conflicts in the Middle East and the unsettled conditions in Afghanistan continue to be worrisome elements in the quest for a peaceful world. The University of Maryland Minorities at Risk Project lists 285 minority groups that could be in future conflict due to different forms of injustice. Over 53,000 UN peacekeepers (military personnel and civilian police) from 96 countries are deployed in 15 missions on three continents.

Yet the vast majority of the world is living in peace, transcultural ethics are being studied, dialogues among differing worldviews are increasing, formal EU and informal East Asia regional groupings of powers are adding to stability, and intra-state conflicts are increasingly being settled by international interventions. The growth of democracy and international trade, the global visibility provided by news media, by the Internet, and by satellite surveillance, and increased world travel and better living standards are all increasing acceptance of the idea that secure conditions for a more peaceful evolution of humanity are possible. Human rights standards are increasing in importance relative to national sovereignty, and the International Criminal Court has begun operations. Once slavery was widely accepted as a "natural" institution; now it has almost vanished because humans changed their minds and institutions. If so for slavery, why not for terrorism and war?

Backcasted peace scenarios should be created through participatory processes, as was done in Chapter 5 on the Middle East. UN early warning systems could be strengthened by involving NGOs and the media to generate the political will to act when local violence and global threats warrant international intervention; advanced intelligence sensors and transceivers could be made available to local citizens so that local realities could be broadcast to the world. More precise sanctions consistently enforced should target elite criminals rather than innocent populations and should create all-party mediation on neutral territory. Strengthen UN and multilateral systems of collective security; identify troops who have been trained together for more rapid UN peacekeeping deployment, with compatible equipment to be marshaled to prevent the escalation of violence. We should study and implement best practices for reducing corruption and collective violence. News media and Internet Web sites could be encouraged to give more balanced coverage that shows positive mediation rather than just scenes of violence. Governments should destroy existing stockpiles of biological weapons, create tracking systems for potential bioweapons assets, and increase the use of nonlethal weapons to reduce future revenge cycles.

The "new security threats" should be integrated into a comprehensive, standardized, and quantitatively based global security index. A world network of CDC-like centers will be needed to counter impacts of bioterrorism. The root causes of the nexus of terrorism-WMD proliferation has to be understood—not just the consequences; public education programs should be created to promote respect for diversity, equal rights, and the value of the individual and each religion. We need to share research on conflict resolution and consensus building that focuses on the common ethical values and oneness that underlies human diversity. Over the long term, education for a more enlightened public and leadership is the answer.

Regional Perspectives

AFRICA: The African Union has created a Peace and Security Council to strengthen multilateral collective security. As many AIDS orphans grow up in crime and teenage population grows, the continent could become more violent. Although some conflicts may have been triggered by environmental degradation, they surfaced as ethnic disagreements or as religious and border clashes.

ASIA AND OCEANIA: Political, religious, and ethnic conflicts and locally based terrorism continue across much of the region. Where is the Afghan heroin money going now? To bypass frozen assets, Al Qaeda and its associates are using alternative remittance systems known as *hawala* and diversifying into gold and diamonds. Middle East water negotiations are the most likely way to build confidence that peace is possible.

EUROPE: Eliminate international small-arms trade or create an international audit system for each weapon. Being party to the ICC should not be optional—in a globalizing world, all world citizens should be accountable to the international community for their acts. People of different nationalities are getting along well, but political and ideological extremists instigate discord. Coalitions based on national politics cannot address global organized crime and terrorism. A global response is necessary. Shared values alone will not do it; a new culture is necessary.

LATIN AMERICA: Colombia continues to be the focus of conflict in the region, while ethnic conflict is minimal in most other places. There is the potential for increasing conflicts between governments and indigenous peoples in the region, as well as cells of Islamic extremists in the tri-border region of Argentina, Brazil, and Paraguay.

NORTH AMERICA: Intelligence technology and military power will not provide security in asymmetrical warfare without genuine cross-cultural understandings and better multilateral cooperation. The knowledge of how to bring about mass destruction through genetic engineering, nanotechnology, and artificial intelligence could have more potential to destroy civilization than nuclear, biological, and chemical weapons.

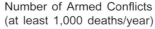

Number of Armed Conflicts (at least 1,000 deaths/year)

Figure 9

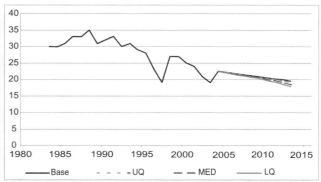

Source: Stockholm International Peace Research Institute, Yearbook 2004, with Millennium Project estimates

11. How can the changing status of women help improve the human condition?

Next year marks the 10th anniversary of the Fourth World Conference of Women in Beijing—the largest UN conference in history. Although it accelerated efforts to improve the status of women, many nations have not fulfilled their commitments to international conventions, declarations, or platforms for improving the status of women in their countries, even though this could be one of the most cost-effective strategies for addressing the other challenges in this chapter. Increasing women's education and participation in the cash economy translates into improved health, nutrition, and education for children, as well as lower infant mortality and birth rates. The World Bank confirms that investing in girls and women is one of the soundest social and economic anti-poverty strategies. Women's presence in UN peacekeeping missions improves access to networks for local women and makes male peacekeepers more responsible.

Meanwhile, violence against females between 15 and 44 years old causes more deaths and disability than cancer, malaria, traffic accidents, or even war. Current reliable global data on domestic violence against women do not exist, but WHO reports that in 48 population-based surveys from around the world, 10–69% of women reported being physically assaulted by an intimate male partner at some point in their lives, and Amnesty International estimates this to be about 33% worldwide. Some 80% of the world's refugees are women and children. The use of rape as a weapon leads to female deaths from preventable diseases, malnutrition, and childbirth complications in war-torn regions across the globe. People newly infected with HIV are now twice as likely to be women as men. Two-thirds of the world's illiterate people age 15 and older are female.

The numbers of women in government and in the cash economy are increasing, as is the percentage of women in all levels of education except in South Asia and sub-Saharan Africa. Women account for 15.4% of parliamentary membership around the world, compared with 11.7% in 1997. Hence it is reasonable to assume that women's status will improve, further contributing to the general welfare of civilization. In the meantime, women earn on average two-thirds to three-fourths as much as men for the same work. In most developing countries, 50% or more of the female nonagricultural labor force is in the informal sector, where earnings and social protection are far less secure.

Future strategies to enhance the status of women should include creating and publishing gender indexes of participation in society, encouraging women to run for political office, guaranteeing the legal rights of women, raising gender awareness in all departments of government, and increasing women's access to resources such as credit, land, technology, training, health care, and child care. Women should establish more networking organizations for women from various economic sectors and geographic regions. This is of particular importance to rural, migrant, refugee, internally displaced, and disabled women. UN Secretary-General Kofi Annan has pointed out that "full equality for women means more than the accomplishment of statistical objectives: the culture has to change." Such an effort includes educating men to fully respect women and also directly working with the media, which too often perpetuates harmful gender stereotypes. Although discussions about the changing role of women are increasing, it may be necessary to explore sanctions against governments that do not guarantee the rights of women. A gender-based Gini co-efficient should be used and publicized.

Regional Perspectives

AFRICA: Rwanda has the world's largest percent of women in parliament (49%), but for sub-Saharan Africa as whole the figure is 14.4%. Though women in many African countries play a substantial role in the agricultural labor force, they are still constrained by their lack of resources and lack of employment opportunities outside of the home due to societal beliefs about women's traditional roles in society. They also generally work more hours than men. This work burden has been further increased due to the spread of HIV/AIDS, as women continue to serve as primary caretakers.

ASIA AND OCEANIA: While 52% of boys in South Asia are in high school, only 33% of girls attend. Poor economic conditions are forcing many Asian women, most notably from the Philippines, Indonesia, Sri Lanka, and Thailand, into domestic or sexual labor abroad. Further, while globalization has brought employment opportunities for many women in Asia, the quality of these positions is often very low. A cultural preference for sons in many Asian countries perpetuates high rates of abortion of female fetuses and child mortality. Despite continued gender bias, programs such as the Grameen Bank and BRAC in Bangladesh and Mahila Samakhya and the Self Employed Women's Association in India have effectively helped empower women. China has begun funding pension plans for parents with daughters to counter male-only child preferences. The increasing dynamism and economic independence of Japanese women has become a social phenomenon. UNDP's *Arab Human Development Report* concluded that achieving legal gender parity was one of the three most important ways to improve Arab conditions.

EUROPE: The status of women in Europe has progressed in the last few years, but subregional disparities need to be resolved. Until men take on more family responsibilities, the quality time of family life will be reduced as mothers respond to social and financial pressures to work outside the home. According to the European Commission, sex trade has increased in Europe, with an estimated 120,000 women and children being trafficked into Western Europe every year.

LATIN AMERICA: Women's organizations in Latin America are currently constructing indexes to measure how far 14 countries in the region have fulfilled their commitments to improving the status of women. Conditions vary widely in the region. About 70% of those entering the University of the West Indies are women, while 98% of abused victims in Bolivia are women and nearly 75% of them did not complete primary school. Governments need to change laws about rape, sexual harassment, and equal pay for women. Despite increased workforce participation, women continue to suffer discrimination in the job market. One of the greatest challenges to the region is changing male "machismo" attitudes.

NORTH AMERICA: Although women in this region have greater legal rights than in most other regions, there is a need to monitor and enforce legislation, remove corporate and government "glass ceilings" to women's advancement, and make special efforts to address women in poverty and drug dependency. Single-mother households are raising a third of the children living in poverty in the United States, which still has not ratified the CEDAW.

Figure 10

Regional Representation of Women in Parliaments
(both Houses combined, as of May 2004)
(world total is 6,302, representing 15.4% of total MPs)

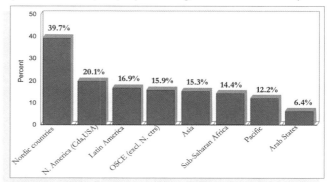

Source: Inter-Parliamentary Union

12. How can transnational organized crime networks be stopped from becoming more powerful and sophisticated global enterprises?

It is time for an international campaign by all sectors of society to develop a global consensus for action. Transnational organized crime has grown to the point where it is increasingly interfering with the ability of governments to act. Nation-states can be understood as a series of decision points that are vulnerable to the vast amounts of money available to crime groups. TOC's power in one country can be leveraged to increase power in others. The IMF has estimated that as much as 5% of the global economy—$1.8 trillion per year—is laundered through the international financial system. This understates TOC's total income, since not all income needs to be laundered. Diversification in diamonds, barter, and other media outside traditional currency systems could put the real income to well over $2 trillion per year. Colombia and Afghanistan have demonstrated the links among TOC, terrorism, and nation-state power. The vast amount of money amassed by TOC allows its participants to buy the knowledge and technology to create new forms of crime to generate even more profits. In addition to government power, daily international transfers of $2 trillion via computer communications make tempting targets. Production of synthetic psychotropes will also be tempting targets in the future.

The World Bank estimates that over $1 trillion is paid in bribes each year; it is not clear how much of that is paid by TOC. TOC has not surfaced on the world agenda the way property, water, and sustainable development have. OECD's Financial Action Task Force has made 40 recommendations to counter money laundering, and the UN has the Office of Drug Control and Crime Prevention's Global Programme against Money Laundering, the International Narcotics Control Board, the International Group for Anti-Corruption Coordination, and the International Criminal Court; nevertheless, there is no international effort on the scale needed.

Information technology could certainly be used to identify sources and target money-laundering locations, create an international agreement to upgrade the recording system for all financial transactions, share information on financial transactions, and coordinate prosecution strategies through an intergovernmental body. The IMF or some UN mechanism might initiate this activity in a special meeting of finance ministers. To make this work, all banks would have to cooperate or be frozen out of the international system. Instant access would have to be available on every financial transaction requested by the international body. Countries would have to give up some sovereignty, as the international body would set the location for prosecution. The international body would authorize the freezing of criminal assets prior to arrest and the transfer of assets after conviction.

The UN Convention against Transnational Organized Crime (the Palermo Treaty) came into force in September 2003. It calls for a variety of modes for international cooperation to help fight organized crime. Possibly an additional protocol could be established to create an intergovernmental body to complement the Global Programme against Money Laundering, with responsibility for identifying money-laundering locations and setting information traps, identifying top criminals by the amount of money laundered, preparing legal cases, identifying suspect's assets that can be frozen and the readiness of relevant institutions to freeze them, identifying where the criminal is currently located and assessing local authorities' ability to make an arrest, identifying the best country in which to prosecute the particular case, and determining the readiness of local courts to move immediately. When everything is ready, this new intergovernmental body would execute all the orders at the same time to apprehend the criminal, freeze the assets and access, and open the court case. Now, how to provide oversight for such a global organization?

Regional Perspectives

AFRICA: Nigeria and increasingly South Africa are the regional centers for TOC. Although not as large a factor as in other regions, links between African rebel factions and organized crime groups are increasing, which is potentially exacerbated by millions of AIDS orphans. Corruption has permeated much of African society and is now perhaps the greatest limit to growth in many countries.

ASIA AND OCEANIA: Human trafficking and sea piracy remain problems in the region. Asian cultures tend to reinforce hierarchical control and loyalty to elders above ethics; hence rigid patterns of crime could be reinforced by societal norms. Decriminalization and state control of drugs, prostitution, and gambling will take the money out of organized crime.

EUROPE: Build on the Southeast European Cooperative Initiative Regional Centre for Combating Trans-border Crime in Romania. Kosovo is now one of the largest channels of smuggling drugs to Europe. If it is not possible to legalize all drugs, then legalize light narcotics and use the tax income to encourage producers to change their profile to useful products or research. Corruption in Western Europe is on the rise, making it easier for organized crime to grow and build bridges to Eastern Europe. Organized crime controls 65% of Russia's GDP, making it the number one security threat to the country. Some say that crime may be a natural part of economic liberalization, as it was in the United States in the late 1800s and early 1900s (although then the scale was much smaller, there were no jet planes, Internet, or weapons of mass destruction, and countries were not being taken over). The task is to find a compromise between corruption and

honesty in the process of privatization and concentration of capital.

LATIN AMERICA: Reduce the opportunities for profiting from undue government regulations that constitute incentives for corruption. The region is the sole producer of cocaine. Organized crime offered to pay Bolivia's national debt to have a free hand in that country. Parts of Colombia the size of Switzerland have already been turned over to organized crime. Few have the courage to fight it, saying that eventually the networks will become legal corporations, but it could also mean they become the political power of the region.

NORTH AMERICA: Would equal numbers of women in senior management positions reduce TOC? Countries must be held accountable for corporations that are involved in criminal activities in their own and other countries. Organized crime should be treated as a national security threat on a par with a strong military threat. Serious change will require a global movement led by activist organizations such as Transparency International backed by reformist politicians, professional organizations, and unions. Governments should legalize "victimless crime" such as drugs and gambling to reduce the cash flow of organized crime. There is a new generation of criminals in the region who are anonymous in cyberspace.

Figure 11

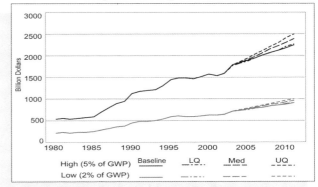

Worldwide Money Laundering Estimates

Source: IMF, OECD, Transparency International, and Millennium Project estimates

13. How can growing energy demand be met safely and efficiently?

It takes 33% less energy to produce a unit of GDP in IEA economies today than it did in 1973. Nevertheless, world energy demand is forecast to increase by 54% from 2001 to 2025 and to require about $16 trillion in new investments by 2030 to meet demands. A Millennium Project international panel has rated funding for commercially available non-nuclear fission and non-fossil fuel sources to generate baseload electricity by 2025 at prices competitive with today's fossil fuels as the most important mission for science and engineering in order to improve the future. The lack of clean and abundant energy has contributed to military conflicts, environmental problems, and poverty. Some 1.6 billion people have no access to electricity, and some 2.4 billion rely on traditional biomass for cooking and heating.

Despite the growth in renewable energy production, without major policy, values, and engineering changes, the global share of renewable energy will be less than 10% in 2025 and oil will still account for nearly 40% of world energy consumption. The world could consume more than twice the amount of fossil fuels over the next 60 years as during the last 60. The impact of greenhouse gases on global warming is cumulative. Developing countries are expected to pass industrial ones in total carbon emissions by 2015, even though their per capita emissions will remain much lower. Unless significant progress is made on carbon sequestration, the environmental movement may try to close down the fossil fuel industries, just as they stopped atomic energy growth 30 years ago. The hydrogen fuel cell R&D competition between the EU, Japan, and the United States may speed development of this alternative to petroleum for transportation, yet fossil fuels and nuclear energy are expected to be used to help make the hydrogen.

Political leaders should declare "abundant clean energy" as a global goal and commit the resources needed. An international fund should be established (possibly by government corporate shares, or national energy per capita or carbon taxes) with the R&D priority of concepts that are scientifically sound, not already being pursued, and too distant to attract venture capital. Key funding categories should be energy for transportation in developing countries; universal access to electricity; carbon capture, separation, storage, and reuse; and the gap between R&D and commercialization. New projects should also include portable sources, energy storage systems, decommissioning of nuclear power plants, and nuclear waste management. All this may require the creation of a World Energy Organization (possibly by elevating the IEA of OECD) to help coordinate energy research, development, and implementing policies—such as the elimination of energy subsidies and tax incentives that perpetuate the status quo and stifle development of alternative sources. Agreement on scientific measurements will be necessary for energy pricing policies to reflect the external and environmental impacts of energy production and use.

Regional Perspectives

AFRICA: Roughly 95% of the hydropower potential in the region is untapped. Carbon sequestration for coal-based power stations and nuclear waste disposal in South Africa is needed. Excluding South Africa, more than 90% of sub-Saharan African household energy comes from wood and other forms of biomass, which contributes to desertification and climate change and undermines health and development. Without increased investments in solar, wind, and hydropower, biomass will continue to be a dominant energy source.

ASIA AND OCEANIA: Demand for energy in developing Asia is projected to double between 2001 and 2025, accounting for 40% of the world's increase. Coal accounts for two-thirds of total energy usage in China, which is a quarter of world consumption—making China a critical player in any carbon sequestration strategy. Supplying electricity to its urbanizing population in a sustainable manner is a huge challenge for China, which should focus more on solar power, wind energy, hydropower, tidal energy, and compressed natural gas for energy sources. Japan and South Korea import nearly all their energy. Japan is studying carbon sequestration for fossil fuels and how to process solar energy in orbit and beam it to electric power grids on Earth. It also plans to have 5 million fuel cell cars by 2020. A Chernobyl-type accident could take place at India's nuclear power plants anytime. The Middle and Near East overlooks the seriousness of the competition to come from alterative sources.

EUROPE: In 2003 Iceland opened the world's first filling station for hydrogen-fueled vehicles and it plans to use geothermal-produced electricity to mass-produce hydrogen within 30–40 years, becoming the first non-fossil-fuel country. Renewable energy accounts for 6% of the EU's energy use, which the EU hopes to increase to 12% by 2010. Electricity from wind increased in Europe by 23% in 2003, compared with a 40% increase in 2002, putting EU Renewable Directive's target at risk. Opinion on nuclear power is divided; Germany has announced it will phase out all nuclear energy production, while France is still nearly 80% dependent on nuclear plants. Inefficient and old coal power and other plants cause environmental degradation and economic loss in Eastern Europe.

LATIN AMERICA: Space solar power satellites may have more allies in the developing world than in the industrial one, with all their vested energy inserts. The region needs to increase its energy consumption per capita, and hence its development, becoming a stronger and more peaceful region. The key to affording enough energy for a better quality of life lies in installing the proper

infrastructure, using more renewable energy sources, and avoiding as much as possible the mistakes made by the United States.

NORTH AMERICA: Require new cars (as of two years after passage of the law) to either have GEM (gasoline, ethanol, methanol) fuel capability or else be fuel-cell or dedicated electric cars; invest in carbon-tolerant alkaline fuel cells that can use methanol as well as hydrogen; and develop low-cost carbon nanotube "molecular sponge" to hold high volumes of hydrogen under relatively low pressure for hydrogen-powered cars. The United States has made the development of hydrogen fuel-cell vehicles (FreedomCar) a national priority, committing $1.7 billion over five years, and announced a $1-billion, 10-year demonstration project to build a zero-emission power plant (FutureGen). Methanol may be the fuel for near-term dual-fired cars and over the long term for more-efficient fuel cell cars. Four options to meet long-range energy demands are fossil fuels, nuclear energy, conventional alternatives, and space solar power. Energy can be beamed to electric grids via microwave from solar cells in orbit or on the moon and from terrestrial sources. Governments need to set deadlines for the transition to non-polluting sources.

Figure 12

Total Primary Energy Supply

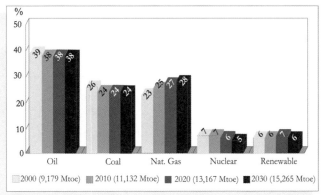

Source: IEA World Energy Outlook

14. How can scientific and technological breakthroughs be accelerated to improve the human condition?

Most people do not appreciate how fast science and technology will change over the next 25 years. The synergies and confluence of nanotechnology, biotechnology, information technology, and cognitive science—or NBIC—will dramatically increase individual and group performance and the support systems of civilization. NBIC products will range from biometrics to counterterrorism systems, from restoring brain functioning and eyesight to increased longevity. E-textile cloths with nanotech threads of antenna, photovoltaics, computation, sensors, ultrasound, and thermal regulation will be worn as a personal early warning and response system. Laser flashes on the femtosecond (10^{-15} second) timescale have tracked atoms rearranging themselves during chemical reactions.

The factors that caused previous changes—such as computer chips, telecommunications bandwidth, new materials, genomics and biotechnology, computational sciences, international standards, and collaborative software—are themselves changing at accelerating rates, with no end in sight. People are surprised to learn that we can see proteins embedded in a cell's membrane tens of billionths of a meter across, that organic transistors with a single-molecule channel length have been developed, that gene variants for schizophrenia, depression, and other mental diseases have been discovered, or that light has been stopped by a yttrium-silica crystal and then released and has been slowed in gas and then accelerated, promising vast improvements in computer capacity. Robot surgery has begun clinical trials, rats' movements have been controlled by remote devices communicating with the animals' brains, an electrocorticographic grid placed on the head of a player using only the signals from the brains has played computer games, monkeys can control a robotic arm with their thoughts, and nearly 13% of humanity is online.

Over the next 25 years NBIC approaches will integrate sciences, engineering, medicine, and business to change the very nature of R&D. They will accelerate efficiency, create better medicines and more nutritious foods using less land and water, and improve learning and mental health. Artificial intelligence with quantum computing will increase collective intelligence, and space sciences will open new technological and social frontiers.

Meanwhile, the risks of some new technologies and scientific developments are enormous, unprecedented, and, many argue, unpredictable. The risks are associated with unanticipated consequences of frontier research or applications and with new weapons applications. (See CD Chapter 5 for global 2025 science and technology scenarios.)

The InterAcademy Panel, a worldwide network of 90 science academies, is increasing access to S&T information around the world; Japan will sponsor the Global Forum on S&T and Society; MIT offers its education materials free on the Internet. Yet more S&T-savvy political and media decisionmakers are needed, who in turn need some kind of international S&T organization to bring together the world's knowledge in a more user-friendly fashion, consisting of data banks of information from many organizations. Such a system could illustrate risks, opportunities, and a range of speculation on items on a cumulative basis. International scientific assessments of biotech and molecular nanotechnology should be conducted, and whatever is found feasible and desirable should be developed on a fast-tracked international basis to address many of the other Global Challenges. Global "collaboratories" via Internet2 should be fostered for NBIC, and transcultural research should be focused on how to improve the human condition. Basic research and development of new theoretical principles must be supported to provide the growing pool of knowledge from which applied science draws its insights.

Regional Perspectives

AFRICA: It will take very serious and conscious efforts on behalf of Africans to make the region part of an integrated global system. Many transfers of technology will be needed from other nations, but production and development should be done in Africa as much as possible to adapt to local conditions.

ASIA AND OCEANIA: China and India are pursuing genetic engineering to increase food supply at lower cost. Societal issues remain unresolved because of a lack of awareness of the benefits of investments in R&D. The region should establish a system linking government, university, and private-sector systems to focus on S&T breakthroughs. In the South Pacific, many governments are pursuing economic rationalist models in which the marketplace will determine the need for S&T. The likelihood of breakthroughs will thus be diminished because strategic research is being neglected in favor of applied research directed at specific problems. Progress in Japanese R&D in robots could help address projected labor shortages.

EUROPE: The mapping of the human genome may be a conceptual breakthrough comparable to the periodic table. To address this challenge, Europe should seek a balance between social and natural sciences and expose scientists and technologists to formal measures of public accountability, include ethical thought about NBIC, and continue foresight programs and communicate their findings to the public. The EU aims to increase spending on R&D and innovation to 3% of GDP by 2010. The needs of transition countries with obsolete technologies include scientific and technology know-how transfer; strategic planning; increased subsidies for the sciences; expanded orientation toward the sciences; and support of the information society, digital economy, Internet, and e-commerce.

LATIN AMERICA: Biotechnology will feed people, cure disease, and eliminate malnutrition. Yet in Mexico the largest tortilla factory declared it would not buy any more genetically modified corn and Brazil has recently eliminated its genetically modified soy by replacing it with traditional soy, so as to become the world supplier of non-genetically-modified products. Many Latin American countries party to the Cartagena Protocol on Biosafety are very active in promoting the transgenic benefits as well as the precautionary measurements.

NORTH AMERICA: The phenomenon of special interest politics has grown from a nuisance to a disaster in US funding of fundamental science and engineering. Is there certain knowledge so essential that free use should override patent law? Rigid control of S&T can drive research underground or overseas. Connect scientific, technological, and ethical education. Genomic information is being disseminated worldwide as it is being discovered, speeding the day when inherited diseases can be prevented. Some believe that North America needs to "digest" these new technologies, not accelerate use of unassessed technologies. Of unique significance for the region is its wealth of innovative/intellectual capacity. The Tech Museum in San Jose offers $250,000 in prizes for technological innovations to benefit humanity (see <www.thetech.org/events/techawards>). Technological development could become a competitive "sport" (e.g., MIT's robot competitions) internally and internationally in order to generate the kind of excitement that produced phenomenal discoveries and lightning-speed developments during World War II and the cold war, but without the destructive component.

15. How can ethical considerations become more routinely incorporated into global decisions?

By addressing the 14 previous Global Challenges through multinational corporations, governments, and a range of international organizations, we add ethical considerations to global decisionmaking. Contemporary entertainment floods our minds with unethical behavior, while news around the world cries out for more ethical interventions. At the same time, synergies of nanotech, biotech, info tech, robotics, genomics, and cognitive science promise god-like powers with ethical implications beyond current discourse. The speed at which we have begun to change the fabric of life seems beyond the ability of science and technology regulators to manage.

Previous moral campaigns by one religion or ideology tend to give rise to "we-they" splits, making it difficult to solve world problems. Collaboration across national and institutional boundaries, as well as religious and ideological ones, seems necessary to address the Global Challenges. Generating the moral will to act across such different systems may require acknowledgment of global ethics. The UN system, the International Organization for Standardization, Transparency International, and the Olympics are unique forces for global ethics. Whether such ethics are discovered or constructed, they are emerging as important to world trade, biotechnology, climate change, countering terrorism, poverty alleviation, etc. Globalization and advanced technology allow fewer people to damage more, in less time, than ever before, hence the welfare of anyone should be the concern of everyone. Such platitudes are not new, but the consequences of their failure will be quite different in the future than in the past.

The prevalence of government corruption, linked with organized crime and terrorism, has become a global phenomenon. Expanding surveillance technology, connected with education and communications systems and the use of universal and accurate lie detectors to counter a range of threats, forces many questions of ethics. An increasingly interconnected world and sophisticated media reporting are making it far more difficult today for unethical decisions to go unnoticed, which seems to call for a new sense of collective responsibility. Much of public morality was based on religious metaphysics, which is challenged by growing secularism; hence, traditional support for morality is weakening.

A global basis for public morality may be emerging, as evidenced by the establishment of the International Criminal Court, corporate ethics indexes, international inter-religious dialogues, UN commissions, think tanks, many ISO standards, and individuals who are organizing themselves around specific ethical issues via the Internet. Others explicitly try to develop global ethics, such as the Universal Declaration of Human Rights, UNESCO's Universal Ethics Project, the Commission on Global Governance, and the Institute for Global Ethics. The largest gathering of national leaders in history issued the Millennium Declaration in 2000 from the UN Millennium Summit as a statement of global values. The UN Secretary-General has challenged business leaders to join the Global Compact by accepting nine principles of global ethics in decisionmaking. The ISO's Advisory Group on Social Responsibility submitted a set of recommendations for the development of deliverables pertaining to social responsibility. Transparency International publishes the Global Corruption Report. Educating children to become responsible citizens will influence adults and thus the entire population. UNICEF estimates that it would cost $7 billion a year over 10 years to educate the world.

A set of universal values or morals from all religions may not be enough to shock us out of our current behavior. Global ethics must not only correspond to the major religious morals, it should also engage both believers and nonbelievers in a new alliance that creates a sense of "being with" all humankind. Courses in ethics should be required for graduation for all levels of school. We have to find effective policies to counter corruption, encourage the will to act (including acting in the interests of future generations), control lobbying, reduce greed and self-centeredness, encourage honor and honesty, promote parental guidance to establish a sense of values, reduce the barriers to the freedom of inquiry, encourage respect for legitimate authority, support the identification and success of the influence of role models, and implement cost-effective strategies for global education for a more enlightened world.

Regional Perspectives

AFRICA: Africa is unable to raise its voice in global decisionmaking due to weak leadership and rampant corruption. A global process should be initiated that leads to an international code of conduct that empowers a multilateral body like the UN to monitor it, including enforcement of international treaties equally among all nations. Corporate boards of directors should be responsible to the community, not just to shareholders.

ASIA AND OCEANIA: The Securities and Exchange Board of India is considering a system that will provide corporate governance ratings for companies. Corruption in India is an ethical problem that has to be solved if democracy is to develop soundly. Developing countries want to catch up with the industrialized West, but many are uncomfortable with free market capitalism and with the West preaching but not leading by example. No serious attention to global ethics is given in Japan; some do not believe there are common global ethics, but that the pursuit to create them is a western notion.

EUROPE: The Wittenberg Center has established five areas of future impact by global ethics: sustainability and global governance, corporate citizenship and new alliances, globalization and international organizations, anti-corruption and integrity management, and discourse among cultures. About 20% of UK's top companies produce environmental and social performance reports, and France, Denmark, and the Netherlands require them by law. Wasting time is a reliable indicator of unethical approaches. Global ethics will become the next big issue after environment in the next 25 years. The European integration process will help establish ethical standards. There is a need to train decisionmakers on ethics and to limit brutality and violence on TV as well as advertisements offering only selfish consumption.

LATIN AMERICA: A new ethical code has emerged involving ecological ethics, human rights, democracy, free-market ethics, and minority protection. But will a new religion be necessary to replace the moral force of old religions?

NORTH AMERICA: Decisionmaking software could prompt the user through ethical considerations of their decisions. The Institute for Global Ethics lists five values identified around the world: respect, honesty, compassion, fairness, and responsibility. Socially responsible investment funds are growing. Ethics and values of the region are highly influenced by a tradition of competition and winning for its own sake. Changes needed include laws against nepotism within the ruling elite, full disclosure, and limits on large corporate and private donations to political fund-raising. Transnational organized crime is the greatest source of corruption.

Global Challenges and SOFI Process

1996 – 97
182 Developments

1997 – 98
180 Developments

15 Issues
with
131 Actions

15 Opportunities
with
213 Actions

1998 – 99
Distilled into

15 Challenges
with
213 Actions

1999 – 2000
Global Challenges

- General Description
- Regional Views
- Actions
- Indicators

2000 – 04
State of the Future Index

2003 – 04

Updating   National SOFIs

Global Challenges
- General Description
- Regional Views
- Measuring Progress

SOFI
- Best and Worst Values
- Developments that Affect SOFI

2.
ASSESSING PROGRESS AND UPDATING THE GLOBAL CHALLENGES AND THE SOFI

The Millennium Project conducted a two-round Delphi questionnaire to improve the assessment of the 15 Global Challenges and the State of the Future Index. The Delphi had the following objectives:

- Receive feedback to update the short descriptions of the 15 Global Challenges
- Obtain suggestions for measuring progress on the Global Challenges
- Collect judgments about the best and worst values for the variables included in SOFI
- Identify and evaluate future developments that could influence the course of SOFI variables

A Global Lookout Panel was created by invitations from the Millennium Project Nodes around the world. The panel's suggestions for improving the general descriptions of the Challenges were used to update the Global Challenges in Chapter 1 and are included in the Appendix of Chapter 2 on the CD. This chapter presents an analysis of the respondents' judgments on how to measure progress on the Challenges and how to improve the SOFI variables.

A complete description of the two Delphi rounds and the responses received is provided in Chapter 2 on the CD.

As part of ongoing efforts to update and improve the 15 Global Challenges, the Millennium Project designed an environmental scanning weblog database system that can be continuously updated by participants. It is described in Chapter 7.

The two-round Delphi invited the Global Lookout Panel to assess the 15 Global Challenges and the SOFI variables. It was structured as follows:

Round One:

- Improve the general description of the Global Challenges.

- Suggest measures that would indicate if sufficient progress is being made to reduce the high priority currently associated with each Challenge.

- Estimate the best and the worst plausible outcomes for the 20 SOFI variables by the year 2013 and the relative importance of each in calculating the state of the future.

- List future developments that, if they occurred, could have dramatic affects on the SOFI variables.

Round Two presented an edited composite list of developments suggested in Round One and asked for judgments about:

- The likelihood of the developments in 10 years

- The magnitude of the developments' impact on variables and the time to reach that impact

More than 250 panelists responded to Rounds One and Two. Demographic charts regarding the participants are presented in Chapter 2 on the CD.

Assessing Progress on the Global Challenges

The Delphi study assessed the Global Lookout Panel's view on how to measure progress on the 15 Global Challenges presented in Chapter 1 by posing the question, *How will we know when progress on this Challenge has been sufficient to reduce its priority?* The participants were invited to rate the importance of the measures provided for each Challenge and to suggest other measures. The highest rated indicators among those given (and the Challenge to which they applied) were:

- The number of people without clean water cut in half (2, water)

- Gender parity in school enrollment, literacy, and access to capital (11, status of women)

- Elimination of laws that discriminate against women (11, status of women)

- Total energy production from environmentally benign processes passing other sources for five years in a row (13, energy)

- International drug smuggling, trafficking of humans, and other income sources for transnational organized crime down by 75% (12, organized crime)

- Corruption down by 50% (15, ethics)

- Ethical business standards internationally recognized and regularly audited (15, ethics)

- Market economy abuses and corruption by companies intensively prosecuted (7, rich-poor gap)

- Number of people living on less than $2 per day down by 75% (7, rich-poor gap)

- Number of people suffering from water-borne diseases down by half (2, water)

- International money laundering down by 75% (12, organized crime)

Although there is much in common between the Millennium Project's Global Challenges and the Millennium Development Goals agreed to by the international community in September 2000, there are three specific areas in which targets of the MDGs can be compared with forecasts produced in this study:

MDG 1. Eradicate extreme poverty and hunger.

Target. Halve, between 1990 and 2015, the proportion of people whose income is less than one dollar a day.

Quantitative Interpretation: The MDG data show a target of 2,320 million people living on less than $2/day by 2015.

MDG 4. Reduce child mortality.

Target. Reduce by two-thirds, between 1990 and 2015, the under-five mortality rate.

Quantitative Interpretation: If the 2002 infant mortality rate of 52.4 deaths per 1,000 live births were reduced by two-thirds, then the 2015 rate would be 17.5 deaths per 1,000 live births.

MDG 7. Ensure environmental sustainability.

Target 10. Halve, by 2015, the proportion of people without sustainable access to safe drinking water.

Quantitative Interpretation: In 2002, about 80% of people in the most populated countries had access to fresh water. In gross terms, the MDG would then place the 2015 target at 90% of the population with access to fresh water.

These MDG targets are indicated on three Figures with an X.

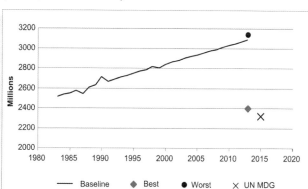

Figure 13

People living on less than $2 per day (billion, without China)

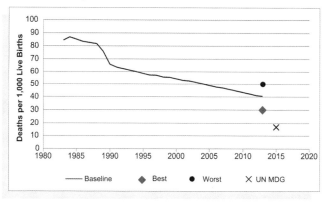

Figure 14

Infant mortality rate

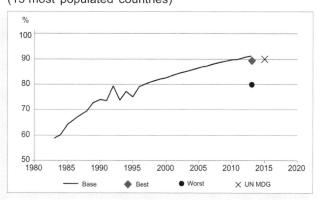

Figure 15

Share of households with access to safe water (15 most populated countries)

GDP per capita, PPP
(constant 1995 dollars)

Figure 16

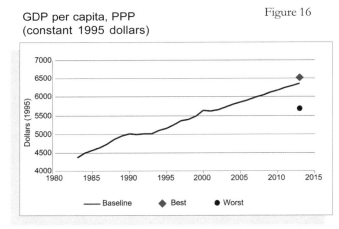

Food availability
(calories per capita in low-income countries)

Figure 17

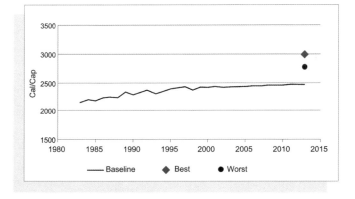

The Global Lookout Panel also provided judgments about the weights to be applied to these measures in a future calculation of SOFI. In this case, the differences between the best and worst cases were small. It had been thought, and is still apparently true, that the weights of the variables depend at least in part on their values; thus the AIDS deaths variable would seemingly be more important if the value of the variable were closer to its "bad" projection (5 million deaths per year) than to its "best" projection (2 million deaths per year). Yet the differences in weights caused by the value of the variable, while in the "correct" direction in all cases but one, were not significant. (Here, the correct direction would mean that the weight of a variable near its "bad" projections would demand a greater weight than if it had "better" values.) A table with these data is presented in Chapter 2 on the CD.

Why did this inconsistency exist? There are two possible explanations that require more study before the issue can be resolved. It may be that the differences between weights of the best and worst values are in reality small, as the group responses indicate, or perhaps the instructions were not clear enough to make this complex concept apparent.

Using only the information about history and the best and worst estimates, it was possible to calculate the level of uncertainty for each variable as:

Uncertainty = absolute (value of "best" – value of "worst")/ 2003 value

Figure 18 illustrates the distribution of "Best" and "Worst" weights.

Weights   Figure 18

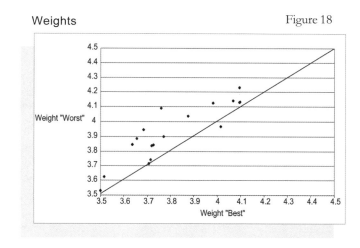

Figure 19 shows the percentage uncertainty associated with each of the variables.

Uncertainty   Figure 19

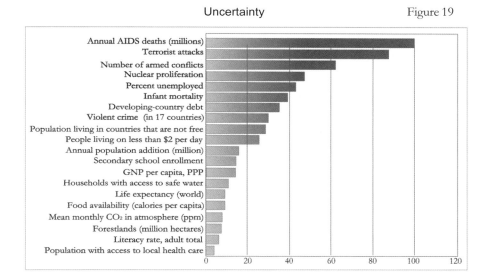

If the judgments about weights were valid, multiplying the uncertainty by the weight would give an estimate of the relative importance of each item.

Chapter 2 on the CD lists all the developments identified by the respondents in Round One as potentially influential in determining the future course of the 20 variables in the SOFI. This list was edited; entries were combined where possible, and these formed the basis for the further inquiry of Round Two. For each item, the panel was invited to rate the likelihood, level of impact, and timing of impact. Some 101 developments were included (some appeared more than once, since they affected more than one variable). The judgments about the developments were then introduced into the SOFI analysis that is presented in Chapter 3.

Given this interpretation, and using average responses, the 10 highest and lowest probability developments are listed in Table 2, together with estimates of the time in years it will take to reach the full impact on the variables with which they were associated.

Table 2: Highest and Lowest Probability Developments

Developments	Likelihood by 2013	Impact Time (years)
Highest Probability		
16.4 New technologies used in detecting criminal behavior; new surveillance micro cameras, psychological profiles, etc.	67.4	7.1
2.6 Degradation/desertification of the soil causing losses in arable land of 3%.	66.5	10.2
5.1 Total industrial output of China plus India grows by 30%.	66.5	10.0
19.5 Telecommunications and medical informatics enable local general practitioners, medics, and nurses to provide increasingly high-quality local services.	66.2	8.0
5.6 Growth of solar, wind power, other "green" energy sources reduces burning in energy production by 5%.	64.4	11.6
2.8 Energy costs rise by 25%.	64.2	6.9
3.2 Nanotech and biotech new industries account for 5% growth addition to world economy.	63.7	8.6
7.5 Economic expansion of at least 5% from new fields such as applied nanotechnology.	63.6	10.7
15.8 Invention and commercialization of new types of arms and surreptitious detection devices used to interdict terror activities.	63.0	7.0
4.3 Global climate causes frequent floods in some regions, polluting the water; drought in others; makes water 5% less available on the whole.	62.6	7.0
Lowest Probability		
2.9 Energy costs drop 25%.	33.1	6.9
3.4 Military/security spending drops 25% from current levels.	36.2	8.5
14.7 International business between North and South is based upon principles of justice and equity.	36.4	12.8
13.8 Conversion of deserts into green lands, adding 5% to global arable lands.	36.9	14.4
15.6 Resolution of Israeli-Palestinian conflict.	38.2	10.6
12.1 Debt forgiveness by industrial world (debt reduced by 50% overall).	39.0	8.3
14.1 Global partnerships for development between rich entrepreneurs and those in areas where people live on less that $2 per day.	39.0	12.4
20.2 Stockpiles of nuclear weapons in the US and Russia further reduced by 90%.	39.6	9.3
1.8 Number of people without safe water throughout the world diminishes by 50%.	43.1	8.4
5.8 Closing of 25% of existing nuclear power plants.	43.2	12.0

Considering the developments as a set, several conclusions can be drawn:

- Despite the difficulty of the questions posed, most respondents provided answers for at least half of the developments.

- Most of the developments were deemed to be plausible: of the more than 8,000 judgments from the Global Lookout Panel about the likelihood of developments, only about 7% were voted "1=almost certain not to occur."

- The distribution of developments, including both those originally suggested and those nominated by the respondents in Round One, shows a skew toward the socioeconomic.

Economic	21.3%
Education	6.8%
Environmental	11.4%
Health	6.2%
Political	15.9%
Science and Technology	14.8%
Social	22.6%

There were many important suggestions made (see the CD Chapter 2 for a complete list). The following list focuses on developments that were both novel and important in the view of the analysts:

- Right-wing politics (on a global scale) reduces access to social services, prenatal care, birth control, and abortion.

- Terrorism or plague affects international shipping.

- Decentralized "home energy production" (renewable energies, solar energy) becomes widespread in industrial countries.

- Industrial-scale use of space resources, solar power satellites, and space manufacturing are in evidence.

- Religious conservatives (pedophile priests, Islamic terrorists, and right-wing media) are discredited.

- High level of unemployment causes weak interest for higher education.

- HIV becomes just another chronic disease; people are less terrified of AIDS.

- Increasingly cashless industrial economies inhibit terrorist funding; increasing surveillance impedes surreptitious activities.

- Planting at least one tree is a duty of any global citizen.

- Terrorists become weapons of mass distraction for politicians.

- Muslim backlash against extremists begins; it becomes politically feasible to silence terror-mongers.

- The presentation of rough violence in media is prohibited in the same way that tobacco advertisements are banned.

- War, guerrilla warfare, and crime might not be distinguishable any more.

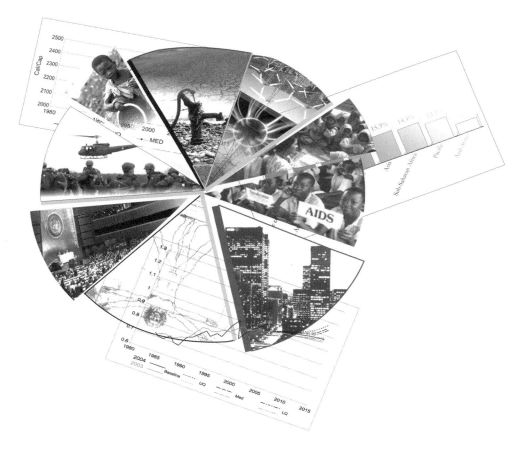

52

3.

STATE OF THE FUTURE INDEX

This is the fourth year in which the Millennium Project has experimented with a State of the Future Index. SOFI is a statistical combination of key indicators and forecasts that depict whether the future promises to be better or worse over the next 10 years. If the promise of the future seems to be changing, then the SOFI is intended to show the directions and intensity of change and to identify the factors responsible.

If confidence were developed in such an index, it could be used for policy purposes: plans could be evaluated and compared on the basis of their impact on the State of the Future Index. National SOFIs could also be created, both for comparison among countries and for internal analyses of the most effective policies to improve a country as a whole. Indeed, several Millennium Project Nodes have indicated that they will construct national SOFIs, and the Venezuelan Node in cooperation with Deloitte & Touche in Caracas has already begun this work (see Chapter 4). In addition, there could be a SOFI for an industry—the future of oil, say—or even one on a particular issue, such as the future of AIDS.

It is important to mention some warnings about aggregate indexes like SOFI. Combining many variables into a single index number can lead to loss of detail about the forces that move the index. Creating an index requires judgments not only when selecting which variables to include but also when weighting them to create an aggregate number. An index of global conditions can mask variations, for better or worse, among regions, nations, or groups. The apparent precision of an index can easily be mistaken for accuracy. For these reasons, many people interested in tracking social or economic conditions prefer to keep separate and distinct the variables that they consider important. Nevertheless, the promise of a State of the Future Index is alluring: it offers the hope of identifying positive and negative changes and points of leverage for policy, as well as of achieving some measure of balance in answering questions about the outlook for the future.

The index can be a powerful global policy analysis tool. For example, in 1998 the Millennium Project examined the interaction among the 15 Global Challenges and found that improvements in one improved the prospects for the others, while deteriorations in one had negative impacts on all the others. This led to the belief that we may learn more about effective policies by studying the relationships among the items in a system than by studying the items themselves. Why not search for the policies that have the most beneficial effects across the set of issues? SOFI provides a mechanism for doing just that. A hypothetical policy can be tested using SOFI, among other techniques, to determine not only whether it promises to satisfy its primary intent but what its overall effect will be on the general future outlook.

Variables Included in the 2004 SOFI

- Infant mortality rate (deaths per 1,000 live births)

- Food availability (calories per capita in low–income countries)

- GDP per capita, PPP (constant 1995 dollars)

- Share of households with access to safe water (15 most populated countries)

- Mean monthly carbon dioxide in atmosphere (ppm)

- Annual population addition (million)

- Percent unemployed (world)

- Literacy rate, adult total (in low- and middle-income countries)

- Annual AIDS deaths (million)

- Life expectancy (world)

- Number of armed conflicts (those with at least 1,000 deaths per year)

- Developing-country debt

- Forestlands (million hectares)

- People living on less than $2 per day (billion, without China)

- Terrorist attacks (number of people killed or wounded)

- Violent crime (per 100,000 population, in 17 countries)

- Share of population living in countries that are not free

- Secondary school enrollment (% of school age)

- Share of population with access to local health care (in 15 most populated countries)

- Number of countries thought to have or attempting to acquire nuclear weapons

The judgmental data used in computing the SOFI this year were derived from a two-round Delphi questionnaire, as described in Chapter 2. The participants in the Delphi study provided their judgments on the best and worst plausible future values for the SOFI variables and their weights. The international panel also suggested and evaluated other future developments that could influence the course of the SOFI variables.

The analysis of the responses showed that the weights for the best and worst anticipated values were judged to be close to each other. It had been our assumption that there would be a greater spread. After all, when a parameter such as food availability is at its worst worldwide, it will gain attention and therefore weight. Careful examination shows that in all cases but one (the share of households with access to safe water in the 15 most populated countries), the worst weight is indeed higher than the best weight, but only by a small margin. We are not yet sure why the differences were small—perhaps it was the way the question was posed—but we have preserved the ability to use both weights in the analysis rather than simply taking the average weight, in case our original hypothesis ultimately proves to be correct.

Judgments about impacts ranged from 1 to 5, with 5= very high impact and 1= no impact.

Respondents were told that negative responses were acceptable. To use these judgments in the SOFI analysis, it was necessary to interpret the panel's responses in terms of a percentage effect.

$$\text{Impact (percent)} = \frac{\text{average of the panel's input-1}}{4 \times (\text{max plausible percentage})}$$

Thus if the average panel judgment about impact were 3 and the maximum plausible percentage were 35%, the equation would yield an estimate of the impact expressed in percentage terms of 17.5%.

The question remains, how can the maximum plausible percentage be judged? This term was estimated by analysts from several sources. First, historical data were examined to observe the largest shifts from a monotonic shape that have occurred in the past. Second, the significance of the projected developments compared with past influences was considered. The table listing the assumptions made about the maximum plausible impact percentage of any single development for each variable within our time frame is presented in Chapter 2 on the CD.

Improvements in the SOFI were made in several ways over the past year:

- Construction of a SOFI uses judgments about future developments that could affect the future course of the SOFI variables. Previously these judgments were furnished by staff; this year the Project's international panel provided these judgments.

- Historical data were updated, better sources were identified, and, where appropriate, new interpolations and extrapolations were made.

- New software was developed to ease the chore of data entry and the computation of the SOFI.

- Sensitivity tests were performed to determine the response of the SOFI to changes in assumptions about two or three key external developments.

- The variable on the number of nations and terrorist organizations having, thought to have, or pursuing nuclear weapons, which had been added to the SOFI set in a sensitivity test last year, was maintained in this year's set, making a total of 20 variables.

A special problem became evident in the analysis of the impacts of developments on the variables. This problem arose from assigning the negative or positive impacts to the developments. There were many cases where the impacts were obviously negative and yet the respondents' answers indicated positive impacts. This might have occurred because the instructions about the option of answering with a negative or positive impact were not adequately emphasized or because "negative" and "positive" impacts could be interpreted as either moving the curve up or down or moving it in a beneficial or detrimental direction.

To handle this problem, the analysts identified which developments obviously had negative impacts. When a respondent gave a positive answer in these cases, the polarity was changed in the analysis. Similarly, a negative answer for one that clearly had a positive impact was changed to positive.

Chapter 2 on the CD shows the full tables with the median estimates provided by the panel (with impacts adjusted as described above) and a table that highlights the developments that were assumed to have negative impacts on the variables with which they were associated.

In all, 101 developments were considered. Some developments appeared under more than one variable; for example, the development "cost of shipping raised 20% due to counter-terrorism and/or disease prevention practices" appeared under both Variable 2: Food availability and Variable 3: GDP per capita.

After converting the likelihood estimates to probabilities and adjusting the impact estimates, a trend impact analysis was run on all the variables and, using these TIA forecasts, the SOFI was calculated. These computations are explained in more detail on the CD. The software used in this analysis is available on request.

The TIA forecasts of the variables are shown in the Figures included in Chapter 1 under the Challenges respectively related to the variables.

The graphs for all the variables are included in Chapter 2 on the CD. Figures 20 to 23 provide some examples.

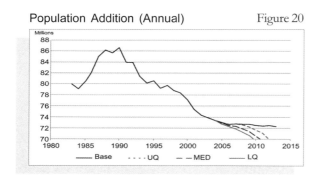

Population Addition (Annual)   Figure 20

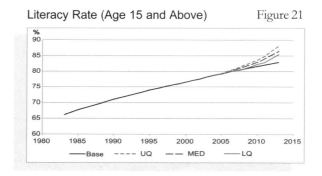

Literacy Rate (Age 15 and Above)   Figure 21

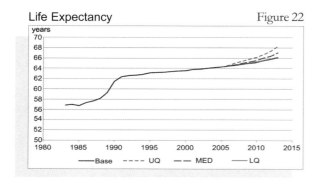

Life Expectancy   Figure 22

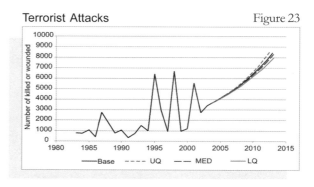

Terrorist Attacks   Figure 23

On June 10, 2004, the US Department of State, the source for the terrorism data, issued the following statement (see www.state.gov/r/pa/prs/ps/2004/33433.htm):

Correction to Global Patterns of Terrorism Will be Issued

After learning of possible discrepancies in the first week of May, the Department of State and the Terrorist Threat Integration Center initiated a review of the data published in the 2003 edition of "Patterns of Global Terrorism." A May 17th letter from Congressman Waxman added impetus to our efforts.

The data in the report was compiled by the Terrorist Threat Integration Center, which was established in January 2003 and includes elements from the CIA, FBI and Departments of Homeland Security and Defense. Based on our review, we have determined that the data in the report is incomplete and in some cases incorrect. Here at the Department of State, we did not check and verify the data sufficiently.

At our request, the Terrorist Threat Integration Center is revising the statistics for calendar year 2003. While we are still checking data for accuracy and completeness, we can say that our preliminary results indicate that the figures for the number of

attacks and casualties will be up sharply from what was published. As soon as we are in a position to, we will issue corrected numbers, a revised analysis, and revisions to the report.

Since the revised figures showed a sharp increase, the forecast is undoubtedly higher than that shown in Figure 23.

Now, taking the historical data for the 20 variables and their forecasts derived through TIA, a SOFI can be produced. (See Figure 24.)

This is a somewhat more optimistic picture than last year, as shown in Figure 25; this optimism results from the new selection of developments and the estimates of their probability and impacts.

A few developments can make things considerably worse. Primary among these is "weapons of mass destruction used by terrorists to kill over 100,000 people." The panel's judgments led to the following assumptions about this item:

- Probability by 2013: 51.33%

- Impact on the variable "terrorist attacks, number of people killed or wounded": 15.2%

- Time for the impact to be realized: 7 years

State of the Future Index 2004　　　　　Figure 24

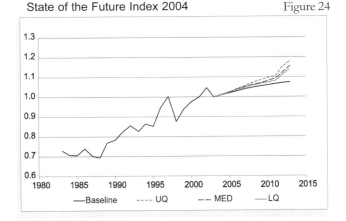

Comparison of SOFI 2003 and 2004　　　　Figure 25

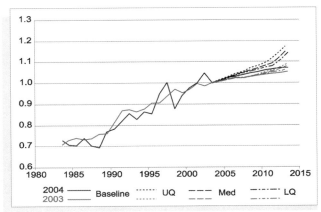

Imagine a worst-case scenario. In one created by the Millennium Project last year in the Science and Technology Management study called "The World Wakes Up," a single individual—a self-proclaimed Agent of God—develops a lethal variant of the Congo virus and in an insane act kills 25 million people over three months (see www.acunu.org/millennium/scenarios/st-scenarios.html or CD Chapter 5.1). Suppose that development 15.2, "weapons of mass destruction used by terrorists to kill over 100,000 people," were changed to bring its effect to 100,000 deaths, as the item indeed calls for. Then its parameters might be:

- Probability by 2013: 51.33%

- Impact on the variable "terrorist attacks, number of people killed or wounded": 1,250% (the baseline for number of killed and wounded casualties in 2013 is about 8,000)

- Time for the impact to be realized: 0.25 years

In that case, the TIA forecast of terrorism casualties would be as shown in Figure 26.

The resulting SOFI is shown in Figure 27.

Finally, we argue that SOFI is a good tool for global policy analysis. Let us try to invent a set of policies that maximize the SOFI.

First and foremost, we would want to reduce the probability of such a terrorist attack; let's say we could, through inspired policy, drop the probability of this development to 10% while maintaining its impact at 1,250% and its timing at three months. In addition, suppose we were to concentrate policy on development 9.4, "developed nations commit the resources necessary to end AIDS and treat HIV," and that this concentration changed the likelihood of the AIDS/HIV event to 75% and its impact to −50% within five years.

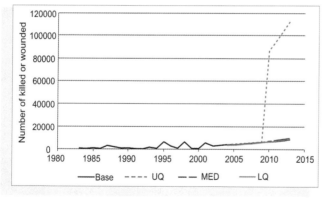

Terrorist Attacks—Modified | Figure 26

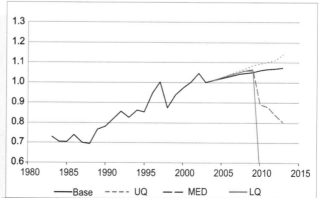

State of the Future Index 2004—Modified | Figure 27

Then:

Development	Orig Prob	Orig Impact	Orig Timing	New Prob	New Impact	New Timing
15.2: Weapons of mass destruction used by terrorists to kill over 100,000 people	51.33	1,250	0.25	10	1,250	0.25
9.4: Developed nations commit the resources necessary to end AIDS and treat HIV	52.6	−4.23	9.5	75	−50	5

And the resulting SOFI would be:

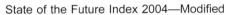

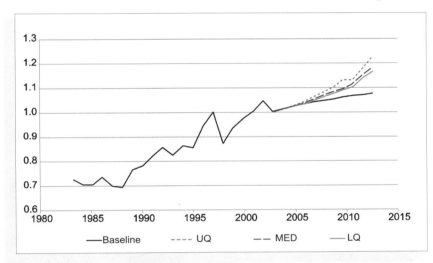

State of the Future Index 2004—Modified   Figure 28

These would be useful policies, indeed.

4.
NATIONAL SOFIs

A new innovation in the evolution of SOFI is its application to individual countries. National SOFIs could help establish priorities for policy and investment decisions intended to improve a country as a whole. This could encourage countries to ask themselves what it means to say a nation is better or worse off in 10 years—and to answer that question in more objective, quantifiable terms. Countries could create their own unique indices for their SOFIs. They could also create standard national SOFIs from the same variables as the global SOFI. Standard national SOFIs would allow comparisons with other countries or events to see if things are improving in one country as much as they are in the world as a whole. Creating national SOFIs also addresses a problem with the global SOFI, which can mask variations among regions and nations.

The World Bank, in cooperation with national authorities, might use these for more-objective loan decisions. Newspapers and other publications could cite or even syndicate SOFI, as they do today with some of the economic indices (such as GDP, HDI, cost of living, and the Dow Jones and S&P 500 indices).

However, it is quite conceivable that the countries or groups should use different variables. For example, two political groups in a single country, working with the same data set, could produce quite different SOFIs by weighting variables according to differing views of their importance and of the best and worst outlook for each variable. Political differences can be quantified in this way. Such applications should be examined in the future.

The Venezuelan Node of the Millennium Project (Jose Cordeiro and Edgar Cotte) together with Deloitte & Touche C.A. (the Venezuelan member of Deloitte) in Caracas took the initiative to build the first national SOFIs for Argentina, Brazil, Canada, Chile, Colombia, Ecuador, Mexico, Peru, the United States, and Venezuela. This study identified new possibilities and problems in constructing national SOFIs. The collection of time series data for the variables proved to be a problem. Data collection at the country level was found to be far more difficult than at the global level. It was impossible to find a usable data set for 8 of the 20 variables used in the global SOFI:

- Share of households with access to safe water
- Number of armed conflicts
- Forestlands
- People living on less than $2 per day
- Terrorist attacks
- Violent crime
- Share of population with access to local health care
- Countries having or thought to have nuclear capacity

For the 12 data series that met the established benchmark criteria in eight countries, 7 variables were found with a complete set of 20 years of historical data:

- Food availability
- GDP per capita
- Mean monthly carbon dioxide in atmosphere
- Annual population addition
- Literacy rate, adult total
- Annual AIDS deaths
- Share of population living in countries that are not free

For the five variables for which the data series were not continuous, linear interpolations were made to complete the required 20 years of data.

The following figures show the results obtained for the 10 countries under consideration. Historical data series are in general very irregular, with the most uniform the curve from the United States and the most irregular the curve from Venezuela. In spite of severe variations during several historical periods of time, all countries show a general tendency toward a better future outlook, but the rate of increase of their SOFI trends is notably higher for the United States, Chile, Brazil, and Mexico as compared with Venezuela, Canada, Argentina, and Colombia.

Chile (Figure 32) and Brazil (Figure 30) show the highest rate of increase in their future outlook, clearly above that for the United States (Figure 37), but note that their non-adjusted SOFI absolute values are significantly below the US values for the whole time span 1983–2012 (see Figure 40). This is an indication that for country comparisons both parameters—the one adjusted to a reference year and the one not adjusted—deserve consideration. This is important since this factor was not necessarily so for the Global SOFI.

National SOFIs may have a significantly higher variability than the global SOFI. With the countries tested, this factor was particularly apparent during the 1980s. The outlook for the future is getting better in the 10 countries analyzed due to a general trend of improvements during the past decade and its effect on an extrapolation 10 years into the future.

Argentina-SOFI   Figure 29

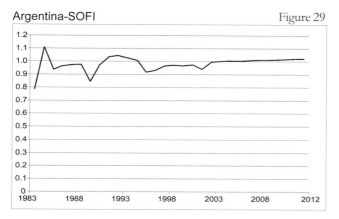

Brazil-SOFI   Figure 30

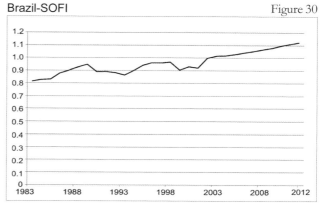

Canada-SOFI   Figure 31

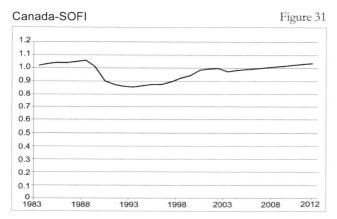

Chile-SOFI   Figure 32

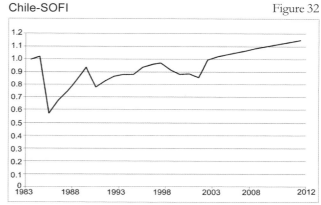

Colombia-SOFI   Figure 33

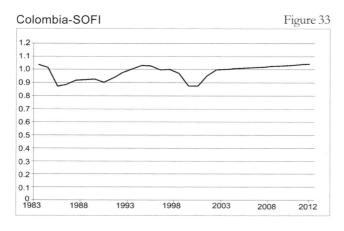

Ecuador-SOFI   Figure 34

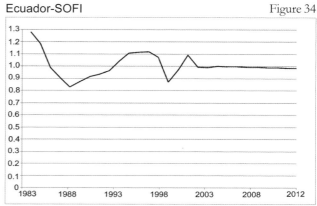

Mexico-SOFI   Figure 35

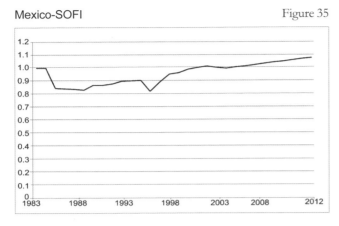

Peru-SOFI   Figure 36

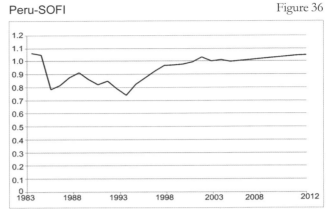

USA-SOFI   Figure 37

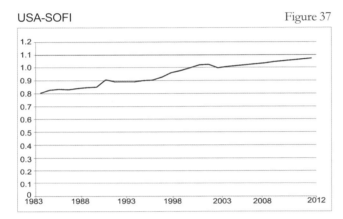

Venezuela-SOFI   Figure 38

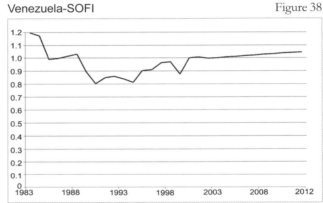

Comparative values of the country SOFIs   Figure 39

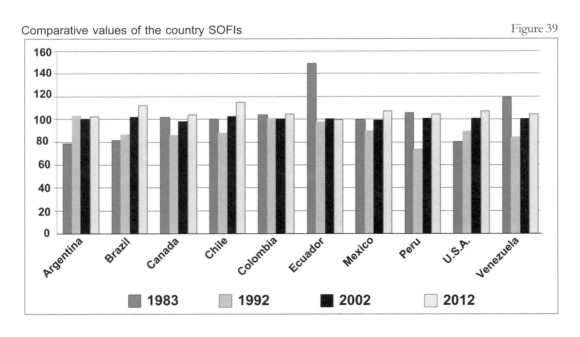

The Global SOFI methodology and its variables are applicable to national SOFIs, but the availability of country-specific historical data for some variables remains a problem. A new effort will be needed to collect a full country-specific database or to find equivalent variables. New sources of data should be identified and data requested from or created by international or national sources. (All statistical computations were performed using the standard SPSS V.12 software package.)

The recent global SOFI work used trend impact analysis, which could be introduced in national SOFIs too, given that possible events or developments in the future could cause great differences among countries. This would challenge countries to identify and assess what future events could alter the trajectory of variables in their country.

Countries' non-adjusted SOFI absolute values

Figure 40

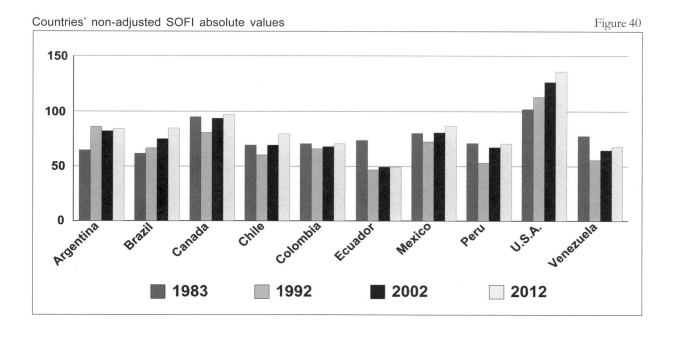

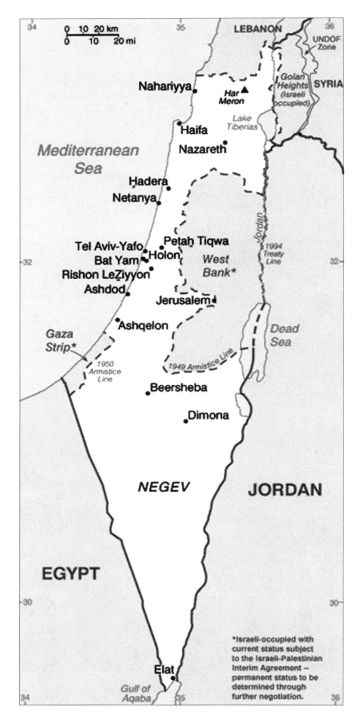

Source: CIA, *The World Factbook*

5.

MIDDLE EAST PEACE SCENARIOS

Anew story is needed for the Middle East.

The old story seems like "bite hands," a game played in the Middle East by two boys. Each puts a hand in the other's mouth. Both bite hard until someone gives up. "Give me justice or I bite harder!" "Give me peace or I bite harder." This chapter provides three normative scenarios, three new stories for the Middle East, that are intended to stimulate and be a resource for new discussions and actions for peace.

The Israeli-Palestinian conflict has to be one of the most studied and contested issues in world affairs today. Surprisingly, there are no well-researched, objective, plausible peace scenarios—not frameworks, in other words, or objectives, analyses, proposals, proclamations, accords, treaties, or road maps, but scenarios: stories with causal links connecting the future and the present like a movie script. It is easy to imagine many scenarios that describe alternative ways the current conflict continues. But what is needed is a set of alternative peace scenarios created by participants with a range of views. In this way, many ideas can be woven together into a story to see how a culture of peace might emerge in the region. The Cairo Node of the Millennium Project at Cairo University in Egypt suggested this void had to be filled by taking a futurist "backcasting" approach to the problem: imagine peace is achieved, and then look at how we got there.

The normative peace scenarios presented in this chapter were created through a unique process. A series of literature reviews and interviews identified seven conditions that seemed required by all sides prior to the emergence of peace. The review also found a set of actions to help establish each precondition. An international panel of several hundred participants was asked to rate the importance of each action for achieving the precondition, the likelihood that the action could occur, and the possibility that it might backfire or make things worse. Additional actions were also collected and rated subsequently in a second-round questionnaire. The results were used to write draft alternative peace scenarios and submitted in a third round to the panel for critical review. The drafts were then edited based on the results and are presented here. Details of the process and results are available in Chapter 4 on the CD.

Scenario 1. Water Works

Now that peace seems to have been finally achieved in the Middle East, everyone is claiming credit for the success. Historians will document the many causes, but most agree today that when the First Lady of Egypt responded to the worsening water crises by inviting UNEP, UNDP, and the Quartet (EU, United States, Russia, and the UN) to be the co-conveners of an exploratory conference on Middle East water, a new sense of hope began to grow in the region.

Since the previous leadership in Israel had said it would take no significant steps in the Quartet's Roadmap until attacks on Israelis stopped, and since the more militant Palestinians had said they would not stop until Israel withdrew from the occupied areas, a new approach had to be found.

Going beyond the mid-1990s water agreements between Israel and the PLO, the Middle East Water Conference concluded that a series of regional water negotiations would be chaired by a UN Envoy appointed by the Secretary-General and funded by the Quartet. The conference would include delegations from Israel, Jordan, the Palestinian Authority, Saudi Arabia, Egypt, Syria, Turkey, and Lebanon, plus the Quartet and observers, and would proceed from the premise that regional water scarcity was inevitable without major desalination; the focus had to be not just redistribution of unsustainable current sources but increased water supply. The US representative stressed this throughout the conference, saying that water-sharing agreements alone would not lead to peace, even if the United States agreed to referee infractions. Producing more water was the key to building trust.

Others believed that the real watershed event leading to peace was the resignations of both Sharon and Arafat, which cleared the way for the establishment of SERESER to coordinate the extraordinarily complex set of agreements, projects, study commissions, joint corporations, and oversight of the fund for joint projects in

cooperative research that evolved over the years. Quiet talks among moderates on both sides produced the Geneva Accords, which led to further quiet talks sponsored by the Quartet that spelled out the conditions for SERESER—a body that took its name from the first letter of seven preconditions for peace: **S**ecure borders for Israel, **E**stablishment of a viable and independent Palestinian state, **R**esolution of the Jerusalem question, an **E**nd to violence by both sides and an effort to build confidence, **S**ocial and economic development, **E**ducation, and **R**esolution of Palestinian refugee status.

Still others said that without secret negotiations by the hardliners, none of this would have been possible. Just as Switzerland provided good offices for moderates to meet in secret and produce the Geneva Accords, Switzerland welcomed the meetings of hardliners, which took a circuitous route getting to the negotiations table.

It all started in Iraq. Sunni Muslims did not want Iraq to become the second Shia Islamic Republic, so representatives of the International Muslim Brotherhood (Sunni) approached the US Administrator in Iraq to offer cooperation, which included efforts to resolve the Israeli-Palestinian conflict. The United States had to give greater emphasis to democratization than military management in Iraq and had to prevent breaking Iraq into Switzerland-like cantons, which would give the Shia the upper hand. Since it was better to have peace with Israel and a democratizing Iraq than an Iran-Iraq Shia juggernaut, Sunni hardliners agreed to meet secretly with Israeli hardliners. The US-Swiss insistence that the meetings begin where the moderates left off in the Geneva Accords delayed the negotiations, but in retrospect turned out to be the only workable framework for them.

Regardless of what historians finally credit as the key trigger for peace, the water negotiations provided a consistent side channel for keeping hope alive. Since water is the most universally recognized human need and the negotiations were more focused than general peace negotiations, they helped to build confidence among the Israelis and Palestinians that peace might be possible. For example, the section of the Wall that enclosed the western mountain aquifer that provides Palestinians in the West Bank with over half their water was rebuilt as a result of the water negotiations. This confidence spilled over into other negotiations in the region, but when these became deadlocked, the Middle East focus returned to the water meetings to restore trust. As water agreements were reached, the Arab Integrated Water Resources Management Network, USAID, the Arab-Israeli joint Regional Center for Research on Desalination in Oman, and UNDP quickly implemented authorized programs, such as emergency water relief systems in Gaza.

The first major success in increasing water supply was the agreement that dramatically accelerated construction of reverse osmosis desalination plants to counter future water scarcity. A commitment to finance the Dead Sea canal and a desalination plant at the Dead Sea to produce water for equal distribution to Jordan, Israel, and Palestine was the first partnership of Israeli technology and Arab oil money. Another agreement followed to build an aqueduct, an irrigation system, and a network of channels from Turkey to Syria, Jordan, Palestine, and Israel. These and subsequent projects have made water available to all today through a common infrastructure for the region. Joint Arab-Israeli educational institutions were established to focus on hydrology, hydraulic engineering, and systems for the transport and distribution of the desalinized water. This also provided the confidence to begin building new oil pipelines from the Gulf to the Mediterranean Sea, with an outlet in Palestine

and another in Israel, which will reduce dependence on geographic pinch points in the Gulf and the Red Sea and will help Palestinian economic development.

Meanwhile, many of the 4.1 million registered Palestinian refugees were in desperate need of education. The collapse of the USSR, the expulsion of Palestinians from Arab Gulf countries, and the closing of most PLO institutions after their forced departure from Lebanon in 1983 meant that access to secondary, informal, and higher education became more and more difficult for refugees. At the same time, the UN Relief and Works Agency had less money to provide refugees with basic services, let alone quality education. The construction of the Wall further complicated access to education, so tele-education seemed the only reasonable course. With UN and EU endorsements, the Palestinian Authority and Palestinian Diaspora gained the political will to raise the initial money from wealthy Arab donor states and personalities to create tele-education programs and initiate an education Peace Corps to support tele-education in refugee camps. As these programs began to show signs of success, such as students getting scholarships to universities and others creating on-line businesses, Israel—as a sign of good will—contributed to expanded operations. This triggered matching funds from Arab countries.

Al-Quds Open University of Palestine and the Open University of Israel jointly implemented the unofficial tele-education program with help from several NGOs and UNESCO, enlisting renowned educators and providing new tele-curricula that emphasized respect and hope for the future. Tele-education reached more women and taught the next generation the value of individual efforts to succeed, since their education was self-motivated and self-paced. Tele-education joint learning activities among Palestinians and Israelis broke down stereotypes, led to enough trust to organize some face-to-face meetings, and increased the commitment and ability to achieve peace in the region.

These developments led to the Great Peace March organized by youth groups. Some of the youth leaders came from the tele-education classes; others were alumni of the Peace Child projects that quietly brought teenagers from both sides together over the years. The youth groups called on the political leaders of both sides to end the hostilities and sign the peace accords, the same accords that later some of these "next generation" leaders would implement as civil servants in the Governments of Palestine and Israel.

While the Great Peace March was being covered by Aljazeera, CNN, and the BBC, the President of Katun stunned the UN Security Council in a closed session by advocating a medical solution: "Diplomatic, military, political, and economic strategies to make peace in the Middle East have failed. It is time to take a public health approach," he said. "All countries have processes to take mentally ill people into custody when they are a danger to themselves and or others, and give them tranquilizers against their will. If so for one person, then why not for two? If so for two, then why not for many?" The Security Council Members could not understand where the President was going with this. He continued, "Clearly much of the Middle East is mentally ill; therefore, I propose that the Security Council authorize a UN force to put tranquilizers in the air and water systems of the conflicting parties until peace is achieved."

No one knew what to say. Was he serious? The silence in the Security Council became unbearable. Finally the President of Katun said: "You know I am right and you know it will not happen. So I propose instead that a UN Peacekeeping Force be equipped with tranquilizer bullets, sticky foam, and other non-lethal weapons and be deployed in areas of conflict or potential conflict." The President pulled out a piece of paper and read: "This UN Force would:

- Enforce the UN General Assembly resolution that clearly defined the borders.

- Oversee the Israeli withdrawal from all areas occupied by it since the 1967 war.

- Protect the Quartet's pollsters who are assessing Israeli and Palestinian views on the proposed borders to make sure that the agreements would survive regime changes within Israel and Palestine.

- Enforce the agreement on religious rights that guaranteed access to holy places in Jerusalem to all creeds."

The UN Security Council approved the recommendations. Within weeks of the arrival of the UN Peacekeepers, SERESER's operations were expanded, all Arab states formally recognized Israel as an independent state, and the UN General Assembly welcomed Palestine as the newest UN member state. Hardliners on both sides of the secret talks in Switzerland insisted that some public process be created to "set the record straight," and through SERESER Archbishop Tutu was called in to help establish a Truth and Reconciliation Commission. The commission, instead of the streets, became the focus of much of the heated debate. And like the water negotiations, the commission became a moderating influence to reduce the violence and to focus on issues of justice. "Town meetings" were held throughout the region to discuss the UN's role. The Israeli delegation in the hardliners' negotiations addressed the Israeli resistance to UN Peacekeepers by getting an agreement that UN forces would have a US commander.

Even before these political agreements were completed, the UN Special Coordinator's Office, or UNSCO, brought together the leaders of the Palestinian Elected Local Councils to design a comprehensive social and economic development process that included self-help participatory planning for local development in the Palestinian territories. People began to assume responsibility for developing their own communities, while seeking external technical and financial assistance.

UNSCO, in coordination with the Palestinian

Authority and SERESER, helped bring in external assistance for this development process by calling representatives together from different international agencies (World Bank, IMF, EU, USAID, UNDP, and international NGOs) and the local coordinating committees representing the Ad-Hoc Liaison Committee, the Local Aid Coordination Committee, and several Palestinian NGOs. Business and religious leaders were also included. New Palestinian leaders who emerged from inter-religious dialogues and the water negotiations earned the respect of their Israeli counterparts, making cooperation possible.

Palestinian Elected Local Councils received training from *Shrouk* (the local participatory planning and development process in Egypt) on how to mobilize local groups of people, help them assess their resources, and plan their future. With UNSCO guidance, this self-help approach attracted resources and expertise. Some Palestinian youth from the United States, United Kingdom, France, and Canada returned to mobilize local Palestinian youth grassroots programs that were financed and launched by wealthy US and Arab millionaires who saw the benefits of bringing young people who had been fully exposed to democratic principles and the Information Age into direct contact with their Palestinian peers. The self-help participatory program ran in juxtaposition with tele-education to supplement each other, and the education Peace Corps and self-help volunteers worked together.

As the local participatory planning processes became more popular, their results became connected to development budget decisionmaking of the Palestinian Authority and SERESER. As Palestinian young people began to see results, their faith in their future increased; this in turn

focused their energy on development of their communities. As a result, Islamic militia groups found fewer volunteers. Natural local leaders emerged throughout the process in each community. Those leaders fed the evolution of representative government based on liberal economic principles. Regular transactions between Palestinians and government officials made the government more accountable to its citizens and provided a trust-building mechanism that was critical to the evolution of democratic culture.

Probably the most difficult issue other than the return of refugees was jurisdiction of Jerusalem. Proposals to declare Jerusalem an international city, establish a UN Trusteeship, and even set up time-sharing arrangements were debated. Finally it became clear that Israel would agree to return to its 1967 borders, including those within Jerusalem, and the Palestinians would agree to give up the right to return to Israel except in special humanitarian situations. All refugees did have the right to return to the new nation of Palestine. All agreed that a plan for peacefully sharing holy sites had to guarantee free access to these areas that would recognize the religious rights of all creeds.

But it was not until a unique process created a time-sharing agreement that UN Peacekeepers could oversee the arrangement. A preliminary "calendar-location matrix" was proposed, which eventually identified all the possible "time slots" and holy sites. It included the times of day when the highest demand locations coincided with the highest demand times of year. Parties who wanted access to the various date/location combinations in the matrix were given the opportunity to rank their preferences from highest to lowest. Each party rank ordered all the cells in the matrix. Initially UNSCO and then SERESER (selected by agreement by all the parties) used the rankings to assign a party to each of the date-location slots. Statements by the respected leadership of the three religions supported the idea and accepted that only a lay administration of the matrix process could lead to an eventual agreement.

There were conflicts, but SERESER used its judgment to complete the matrix. Some seemingly impossible impasses were solved by giving jurisdiction for alternating years. Others were resolved by the special lay committee for ongoing disputes. Once the master calendar-location matrix was filled in, it was made public for final commentary. With minor modifications, the final Jerusalem Matrix is still used today.

One factor that helped heal the region was the Arabic television series "Salaam-Shalom" about two girls—one Palestinian and one Israeli. They met in a peace camp and made a pact to counter the hatred in their communities. Although the Peace Child exchanges between Palestinians and Israelis included only a small number of teenagers, it did stimulate conversations on both sides that added to the belief that peace might be possible one day. The idea was approved by the hardliners' talks in Switzerland, which, it was rumored, even suggested several story ideas.

Each week the girls on the television show confronted seemingly impossible obstacles, and each week they overcame them with extraordinary compassion and intelligence. Television sets across the world showed how the girls used cell phones connected to the Internet to create mini swarms of sympathizers who ran to the area and overwhelmed an impasse. "Copycat" peace swarms began to appear in the real world. Young people armed with their "peace phones" started to call everyone in their areas to calm emotions at checkpoints and other areas of confrontation.

Almost immediately after the first few peace swarms, a Peace Phone Internet weblog and photo gallery was set up, opening a worldwide window on the process and creating a near-instantaneous "global fair witness" to the outcomes of each swarm. The "before" and "after" photos on the weblog, together with the weekly "Salaam-Shalom" television shows, added global pressure for more rational negotiations that finally drew the lines for peace.

Radio talk shows were alive with discussions about each TV program. The one most vigorously discussed had the girls creating a peace swarm to support Archbishop Tutu's suggestions on how to establish a Truth and Reconciliation Commission. As "Salaam-Shalom" was recognized as a successful television series, an adults' version followed that had politicians and other leaders challenged to solve more sophisticated problems of balancing peace and justice. Dismantling settlements in the West Bank nearly caused a civil war. The Wall took a longer time. Both transitions were helped by the active involvement of the media and the Truth and Reconciliation Commission.

With the evolution of democratic processes in the region and continued security guarantees from the United States, Israel surprised many in the Middle East when it ratified the Nuclear Non-Proliferation Treaty as a gesture of long-term good will and allowed IAEA inspectors to verify their dismantling of nuclear weapons. These actions led even the skeptics to nod their heads and say that this time maybe it really would be a lasting peace.

Source: worldatlas.com

Scenario 2. The Open City

The white smoke signaled the election of a new pope. He assumed the office with humility and fervor. His priority, he announced, was facilitating peace around the world, particularly in the Middle East. He began his mission by addressing the Jerusalem question. Although his advisors cautioned "you can only blunt your authority—it's unsolvable," he maintained that God had given him this mission and as far as he and the church were concerned this took priority over politics. "The fact that it is a difficult mission," he said, "only raises the stakes of the test. Is it more difficult than the tests that God gave Jesus, Moses, or Abraham?" The cardinals were mute but whispered among themselves, "the church will be in chaos."

He personally called the leaders of the Jewish orthodox and reformed sects in Israel and their counterparts in the Muslim world, as well as Buddhist and Hindu leaders. (The non-involved religious leaders were invited to provide added credibility to the proceedings.) The new US president and EU leaders gave secret and subtle signals that they endorsed such a meeting. Deft use of the media—particularly live interviews on CNN and "60 Minutes"—made it hard for the religious leaders who were invited by the pope to refuse to meet and talk.

When the plans were made public, Muslim hardliners called this a "new Christian crusade." Jewish right-wingers were also not very interested in the views of the Catholic Church, recalling the expulsion of Jews from Jerusalem during the Crusades.

Yet the meeting plans continued and the religious leaders met on neutral ground, at an isolated ranch in New Zealand, and called their historic session Religious Leaders for Peace, or RLP. That the Chief Rabbi of Israel and the Grand Mufti met in the same room was viewed as a worthy accomplishment and a milestone in its own right on the way to peace, since attending the meeting carried the very real risk of being ostracized by conservatives in their own camps.

At the first meeting, the initial coolness worsened a bit after each member justified his or her position as God-given. Then the pope said, "Yes. God has blessed each of you as you have said, and he has also given us brains with which to reason, and that is what I pray we can do. This issue of Jerusalem pertains to religious law and custom; it should be above secular self-interests and politics and we can at least begin to discuss how to resolve it. It is too simple to say that Jerusalem can be a city-state like the Vatican; there are three religions involved here. We must ask God for guidance."

Perhaps the meeting went ahead because Jews, Palestinians, and Arabs were war-weary; perhaps the governments realized that the possibility of progress without some help from outside was not good; perhaps it was the general belief that the issue had progressed to the point of being "much too important to be left to governments"; perhaps the rise of interest in religion around the world caused people to be open to considering "a higher way."

The religious leaders began with points of agreement: free access to the holy sites should be guaranteed. How ludicrous it would be, they agreed, if one religion were to attempt to deny access to anyone of another religion who wanted to pay homage there. The plan must be beyond political, ideological, and economic interests. It grew from these seeds of agreement. Jerusalem should be an open city under no nation's sole jurisdiction, but under religious protection and authority. They recognized that the problem of Jerusalem does not affect just Israel or a future state of Palestine but is of global concern. Their proclamation recognized that Jews, Muslims, Christians, and other faiths have to work toward a sharing of God's gifts.

But the question before the group was how to proceed.

- One participant pointed out the UN had already laid the foundation. In late 2003, a UNESCO conference had noted that two of its resolutions had strong support from both Israeli and Palestinian representatives. The UNESCO participants "reiterated their support for the initiative taken by the director-general to prepare a comprehensive plan of action to safeguard the old city of Jerusalem (al-quds); and invite him to send as soon as possible, in cooperation with the concerned parties, a technical mission and to establish, within a year, a committee of experts 'entrusted with proposing, on an exclusively scientific and technical basis, guidelines for this plan of action.'"

- Several participants argued that each group—Christians, Jews, and Muslims—should have definitive borders in the "old city" based on their history and tradition.

- Other participants focused on governance issues: a subgroup suggested that the city have a constitution and a representative administration, involving the three religions but also including a UN representative with a double vote for five years or until normalization without the UN presence could be achieved.

- Another acrimonious issue: some of the delegates felt the Temple Mount should be an "open area" not belonging to any jurisdiction; others said that the open city idea would not work because of problems of security, customs control, and so on. They argued that the UN failed in 1947 to enforce its plan for internationalization of Jerusalem, and it was not plausible that such a plan would succeed today. It was an idea whose time came—and went.

- Finally, some people said they wanted no part of the UN at all but suggested another international organization be created for these purposes to establish clear goals with respect from all the actors and with plain

authority to carry out the results of the negotiations and make them permanent.

When the debate seemed endless and agreement elusive as ever, the pope moved the group for prayer at the holy sites, at the Holocaust Memorial in Jerusalem, and at the graves of Palestinians, and asked that the religious leaders pray for forgiveness of violence, for wisdom, for the spark of leadership, and for the insight needed to form a plan. It was a poignant and catalytic moment. A plan was drafted and the leaders pledged to maintain contact and work under their God for peace.

The Religious Leaders for Peace report that emerged from the meeting was directed to the Secretary-General and asked that the UN General Assembly enact a resolution to declare Jerusalem an open city of a new design and that the governments of affected nations support the plan with required legislation. The UN's role would be codified by the UN General Assembly and Security Council resolutions. Under this plan, Jerusalem's leader would be elected every six years by the General Assembly, with the rule that no sect would have control for more than one consecutive term. Terrorism in the area would be dealt with harshly.

Publication of the RLP conference recommendations evoked widespread public acclaim and a few pockets of dissent and grumbles of "sell-out" and worse, but it was clear that the weight of public sentiment had begun to build an unprecedented momentum for peace. Even the most extreme factions felt the ground shift under them; what God wanted was now redefined.

Religious leaders around the world discussed the potential consequences of RLP. Although they did not put it so directly, the mullahs, mashaikhs, and orthodox rabbis in the Middle East faced a central issue of preserving power and face.

For the mullahs, there were new arguments. Muslim believers had long said that all of Palestine was given by Allah to the Muslims. Yet a holy man said the Jews had a right to be in the Middle East as surely as we ourselves do. The holy Qur'an tells us of the Promised Land for Jews. It says that God had promised the Holy Land to Moses and his followers on their way out of Egypt (the Qur'an 5:20–21), so Muslims cannot casually dismiss the concept of the Promised Land. Muslims need to develop methods to attract Jews to come back in a way that is not threatening to Arabs and Muslims. Imagine if Egypt, Syria, Lebanon, Iraq, and Jordan could develop policies and provisions that say:

> *We would welcome any Jew who wants to come to this part of the world, being part of the promised land, to come and live, we'll give you citizenship; you want to buy a house, buy land—fine; you want to have your relatives come live or visit, fine; do your work, live with your community, build your synagogue, have your own laws to govern your family and community life. But do not threaten a national entity. And come to any part, come to Syria, come to Egypt, come to Iraq, and come to Jordan, whatever you believe the promised land to be.*

Such a solution would be based on a religious understanding of God's promises to Jews and Muslims alike. And he added: without intending to be cynical, we can expect in return from the Jews an equal admission of the right of our displaced people to return to their homes as well.

Turmoil. Chaos. Other Muslim clerics interpreted the holy word in their own ways but no matter what spin was put on the proposition, Qur'an 5:20–21 was clear enough and could not be rationalized away. Terrorism needed to be declared a religious crime. The threat of a fatwa for those who disagreed helped end the suicide bombings. Some extremists said that they would continue, that violence worked, that the holy Qur'an could be read and interpreted in different ways, but the die was cast and the momentum for peace built.

In Israel, orthodox rabbis who steered the far right were at a loss. By providing a religious basis for the Jews to exist in the area, the Muslims had, in a single stoke, eroded the political power of

the Israeli far right. Check, maybe checkmate. The rabbis issued this statement:

> *Jews accept that the way to fulfill the promise of God does not include depriving others of their homes; and if Muslims and Arabs recognize the sincere attachment of Jews to the promised land and make serious efforts to accommodate that promise...we are in for a "deep peace," not a superficial one that has been broken, stepped upon, and tarnished, for 55 years. We vow to extend the Jewish idea of the sanctity of the home to others and will help bring about a future that makes homes—all homes—holy and safe.*

The idea that started in New Zealand among religious leaders took on political reality: the retaliatory bulldozing stopped. Religious leaders urged that seek-and-destroy missions be put on hold, and they were.

The fanatics did not yield immediately. From one side: "We will bomb until Israel topples." And from the other: "We will retaliate with all our strength—we were weak once and it cost 6 million lives." Yet slowly the power base of the extremists eroded as it became clear that support was disappearing, and they gradually became irrelevant. In Israel and the future state of Palestine, a movement toward secularism accelerated.

Against the background of improving conditions (removal of the Wall, a workable social net for Palestinians, ending of the killings), education of young Muslims changed. The schools that once taught hatred for the Jews moderated, turning to if not enthusiastic tolerance, then at least an acceptance of laissez faire—a reasonable first step for moderates on both sides. The schoolbook texts damning Israel were withdrawn;

in their place were books teaching tolerance and the positive elements of each religion's work in the region. This so-called Cordova program was launched by three Arab countries (including Syria and Egypt) and was based on the successful collaboration of all three religions under Spain's Moorish golden age in the tenth century to teach tolerance, cooperation, and the values of a "win-win" peaceful world. Exchange programs were extended to provide education for teachers in other settings—Israelis in Arab universities, Arabs in Israel. Schools in the region were created to teach both Arab and Israeli children. To change from hate to tolerance could not be instantaneous, but it began with the hope that the new generation would do better than the old and would carry visions of peace into adulthood.

With RLP, the UN mission, the diminished teaching of intolerance, the acceptance by many Muslims of the idea of a Jewish presence in the Middle East, the end of suicide bombings and the retaliation they evoked, and the softening of the teachings that had inflamed rather than calmed, all that remained was to cement the nervous peace that existed.

With violence from both sides almost at an end, a tenuous ad hoc confidence was built from the bottom up through hundreds of thousands of projects and business ventures that involved both Muslims and Israelis. The projects were large and small (from agricultural cooperatives to jointly owned shops), local and national (from new schools open to all students to lower import and export restrictions between Israel and Arab countries). And with this improved spirit of confidence, the ventures grew in number and significance, economic development grew, jobs became plentiful, unemployment dropped, and in a marvelous demonstration of social feedback, nascent prosperity bred more confidence and cooperation. Travel into and out of Israel was normalized, controlled only by passports and visas. A NAFTA-like free trade zone was established (covering Israel, Palestine, Lebanon, Syria, and Jordan) to improve the competitiveness of

the region in the global economy, to decrease dependence on outside big powers, and to help transform domestic economies. In addition, expatriate communities of Jews and Arabs established functional ties aimed at making this new pan-Middle East a reality. Through investment, leadership, and pressure, expatriates became a powerful force that moved the process forward—to the benefit of their nations and of their nations' businesses, economies, and people.

Outside observers marveled at how the need for employees eradicated the prior need for travel restrictions. It was only possible, they said, when the end to suicide bombings and retaliation was a credible fact. Some years ago, someone had said, "End the suicide bombings and the response to them and everything is possible." He was right.

A joint project sponsored by international Christian aid agencies, Arab oil sheiks, and Jews around the world contributed not only to the elimination of poverty in the region but also to growing religious and cultural understanding. A special Israeli-Palestinian fund was also established for reconciliation; thanks to this fund, victims of torture and arrests and the families of people killed by the army and terrorists of both parties obtained compensation.

It would have been too much to hope that all violence ceased as if a switch were thrown to move from darkness to light; even in the most peaceful setting there are violent people. And so it was in the Middle East. But now nations and their people disavowed isolated acts and labeled them inhumane and counter-religious.

In a year of growing economic cooperation, an Israeli-Palestinian commission was appointed to review the status of refugees. They negotiated an agreement specifying a particular number of Palestinians who would have the right to return to Israel and of Israelis who could remain in the Palestinian areas. Israel argued that this limitation in the number of migrants was in fact no different from any country setting immigration limits. Palestinians responded by saying that Israeli limits would keep people from the locations of their birth and their families. The Israelis were clearly concerned about being outvoted by the immigrants (Palestinians called them "repatriates") in their democratic society. The issue promised to be inimical to the process, but compromise was finally reached by accepting a limit based on census data that recorded ethnicity and by restricting the vote to people who had lived in the country for more than seven years. In addition, should a Palestinian state be established, Israeli settlers in Palestinian areas and Palestinians living in Israel would be given the opportunity for dual citizenship.

Post-Arafat, post-Sharon politicians followed their vocal populations. A historic proposal came to the UN from Israel, based on discussions and contributions of Israeli and Palestinian constituents. There was skepticism about requesting a role for the UN, but in fact there was nowhere else that this proposal could be made. It rested on the tradeoff between the need for Israeli security and the need for a permanent Palestinian state. Israel agreed to withdraw from all areas it had occupied since the 1967 war, to close appropriate settlements, and to cede these areas to the new state of Palestine. Israeli settlers in the areas would be given dual citizenship. It called for the free and open recognition of an independent Israel by all Arab states, with a sovereign right to exist in perpetuity. From the Palestinian point of view, the recommendation clearly defined the borders of the newly proposed state (roughly as in the Geneva accords). Since the Palestinians had participated in the definition of the resolution, it was clear that the recommended borders would be acceptable. The resolution also called for enforcement by the UN (a much debated point) and defined sanctions and penalties for violation of the provisions of the resolution. In a move never seen before but perhaps reflecting a pattern for the future, the resolution was ratified by a plebiscite, helping to ensure that when the agreement was accepted by the UN it would be supported by people in these countries.

Extremists on both sides attempted to derail the plebiscite and the agreement and to intimidate people through various atrocities. But these just caused the public to revile extremism even more, and the vote approved the resolution overwhelmingly.

Thanks to the economic boom, the successful peace process, and the growing political culture, both Palestine and Israel became islands of democracy and prosperity. The beneficial influences flowing from them contributed to profound political changes in the Middle East. The situation in Lebanon became much more stable thanks to the return of Palestinian refugees to Palestine and Israel and to the dismantling of militia such as Hezbollah. Muslims and Christians in Lebanon followed the good example of Palestine and confirmed the peace treaty; Lebanon became the prosperous country it used to be.

And the mullahs, mashaikhs, and rabbis, reflecting on the events since the RLP conference, said it was God's destiny. The rest was details. Inshallah.

Scenario 3. Dove

In Israel, it started with a simple idea: end the retaliatory violence. The plan was code-named Dove. Israeli leaders debated the possibility in secret; the debate occasionally became public for a short while in the Knesset, but by and large it was secret. The idea of Dove was to turn world opinion, possibly even the preponderance of Palestinian and Arab opinion, against the idea of suicide bombings. The hawks of the argument said, "There are only two responses to the violence of bombings: 'Turn the other cheek until they tire of killing us,' or 'An eye for an eye.' The Talmud teaches the 'eye for an eye' approach; our public and the world will think us weak if we abandon it; the enemy will see our turning the other cheek as a sign of capitulation. We must continue to respond even though it is a dark tunnel we go down." Their opponents said, "But in history, 'an eye for an eye' was meant to limit retaliation, not escalate it: so that a small injury only evoked a small response. We have tried the club and as you say it has only led us down the dark tunnel where our only alternative is stronger force. We drive them into a corner with our escalating retaliation. If we were to just stop—unilaterally announce it—the world would see the Palestinians in a new light. Now they are seen by many people as freedom fighters simply because we respond. If we stopped they would soon be seen for the terrorists they are. And perhaps if we stopped, moderate Muslims would rally and take the initiative to press for peace on their side."

While that secret Israeli debate was going on, Islamist extremists had their own secret debate. The coincidence in timing was extraordinary— perhaps it was simultaneous exhaustion on both sides that led to these secret internal discussions. The Islamist hawks argued for increasing the scale of their activities, moving from high-explosive missions to other lethal forms that would involve more people and thus become

even more visible, frightening, and persuasive to the Israelis. The forms that might be used were obvious enough and easily available: from chemical and radioactive toxins to small nuclear weapons. They said: "Don't the Israelis know that suicide bombing is our only effective weapon? They must realize that scale is important to our cause. Just consider how effective the operation in New York was in disrupting the West and changing the nature of the conflict. We brought it home to them. Our cause is now on the minds of all people around the world. It unleashed immense forces that can only lead to our victory. Measure our success by the West's frustration in Afghanistan and Iraq, by the spread of global terrorism, by the impotence of the UN. We must keep faith in our ultimate victory."

Their opponents in this argument were radical in the opposite sense. They said: "Consider what you have said. Our actions have wakened the sleeping giant. Libya has capitulated. UN inspections are starting in Iran. We are hiding in Afghanistan and Iraq. Does this lead to our goal? Does this help us to establish our own safe homeland and the condemnation of Israel for its misdeeds?" The response: "How you have changed, brother. We used to say it was our mission to eliminate Israel and take back our homeland, now you're willing to settle for condemnation."

"Yes, perhaps this argument is a bit different from before, but it recognizes a reality—Israel will not be eradicated. The West will not permit it. Do you not see how our present course works to the disadvantage of establishing our own homeland? It is costing us the best and brightest young people who could be the leaders of that country. If we desist, if we change tactics, then who will be seen as the aggressors? Who will fare better in any negotiations? What excuse will their Prime Minister then have for breaking our homes and killing our people?" The response: "But can we stop the suicide bombing even if we wished? Would we have to gun down our own people?" The question hung in the air.

So each side had its reasons for wanting to stop and turn to a new path but, like the sorcerer's apprentice, the momentum carried the bombings and escalating retaliations on and on.

Then an unexpected event changed the tide:

Israeli Refuseniks Say They Will Not Participate in Bombing Attacks

Israeli press, public, and politicians condemn 27 pilots as unfit to serve

JERUSALEM - Twenty-seven Israeli reservist pilots last week joined the "Refusenik" movement, saying they would not participate in bombing attacks in the West Bank and the Gaza Strip, which often injure civilians. "We refuse to participate in Air Force attacks on civilian populations," the pilots said in a petition delivered to the head of the air force, Maj-Gen Dan Halutz. "We refuse to continue harming innocent civilians."

Last week's Refuseniks are part of a small but vocal movement opposing Israel's policy of "targeted killings," in which helicopters and planes drop bombs or fire missiles to kill terrorists hiding in civilian areas.

This was part of a peace movement—"small but vocal," Reuters said—not generally known outside of Israel. In fact, moderates in both the Palestinian and Israeli camps had been in contact for some time. They talked on an Internet peace site, usually using pseudonyms; they said peace was achievable, a remarkable statement to be made when killing and retribution were all around them. History, they said, will condemn us for not taking a position and acting on our moral convictions. Life as it is today is unacceptable.

The movement was visible outside of the region. The idea that moderates might gain power and that this new force might help bring peace was enticing. The unspoken question at the UN, in Washington, in London, and everywhere people of good will searched for peace was, "What can be done to encourage this movement?" Within Israel, within the ranks of the Palestinians,

there was opposition, of course. Peace movements such as Mothers for Peace in Israel had come and gone—were times different now, would one killing, one murderous bomb, one ill-conceived assassination tip the scale? Some hoped it would; some feared it would. At the UN, the newly established Gandhi award recognized the moral courage required to call for moderation. Because it could make the recipients targets, it was given anonymously, with the announcement delayed until peace was achieved. The United Nations established an Academy of Non-violence as a permanent institution. The Refuseniks, who were arrested for resistance against military authority, were adopted as prisoners of conscience by Amnesty International. A wide-scale movement for their liberation was initiated, and finally they were released from military prisons. Their leader was nominated for the Nobel Peace Prize, but the principal reason for progress was that each side could say: "See, there is a partner on the other side."

The refusal movement came at the same time the politicians were searching for a way to change course. These forces came together and steps, at first tenuous, moved the violence toward peace. Following the practices of Gandhi and King, the movement grew and, in echoes of the Vietnam era, when dissent grew in the United States and politics followed, dissent in Israel and among Palestinians became mainstream.

Here's what happened next. It was like a chess game. Leadership on both Israeli and Palestinian sides changed as a result of many factors: increasing external political pressure, new elections, aging of the principals, and political infighting all played a role. Popular support grew on both sides, spreading from the vocal Refuseniks to the broader population. With the new leadership in place and the movement toward peace swirling around them, the game moved forward. The Israelis got a guarantee that the bombing would stop and the instigators would be arrested and punished. The Palestinians got an ironclad agreement that the Israelis would withdraw to the pre-1967 borders, end building new settlements (existing settlements could remain, with dual citizenship for their populations), and stop the retaliatory raids. The Palestinians called it an end to occupation. The Israelis called it a victory for peace.

Within months, the Israelis negotiated a series of treaties and agreements not only with the Palestinian Authority but with essentially all Arab states, stating that Israel had a right to exist and that there would henceforth be a state of non-aggression in the area. Palestinians and neighboring states welcomed Israel's agreement to sign the Nuclear Non-Proliferation Treaty in return for their own promise to remain non-nuclear and allow international inspections under the UN.

Other problems still had to be resolved in this game of give and take. First was jurisdiction over Jerusalem (eventually it became on open city, with its own democratic government, open to all religions, with responsibility to guard and protect all holy sites). Second was the problem of Palestinians who wanted to return to Israel. Israel perceived that an avalanche of migrants would upset the political structure; as a result, immigration quotas were established. Lebanon, Jordan, and, to an extent, Egypt and Syria, helped by absorbing some of the migrants. Cynics searched for hidden agendas but peace was in the air. The extreme Muslim minority became invisible and this was a matter of concern, but conspiracy theorists aside, the silence was welcome.

As this give and take progressed, both the United States and the EU stayed back from direct participation but helped in other ways. Foreign capital flows into the region were encouraged through trade and capital incentives. The United States mounted a diplomatic campaign to defuse Arab financial support of the militants and it slanted its support for Israel away from arms. The rationale for these policy shifts was simple: for a constructive Israeli-Palestinian process to unfold, outsiders needed to stop feeding the fire. Some politicians wanted to "help" the process along in other ways (and reap some political benefit), but wiser heads prevailed and the two parties were largely left to work out the agreements themselves.

When it was clear that the chess game was evolving, foreign capital did flow into the area, as had been hoped. New businesses were established, and unemployment among Palestinians dropped sharply. It was a self-fulfilling cycle: the move toward peace sparked the environment for peace. With new large-scale water projects, large portions of the Negev Desert were made fertile and habitable.

And the crown jewel: both parties presented a formal joint statement to the UN Security Council, declaring that they considered resolutions 194, 242, and 338 fully realized and asked that the UN monitor for a time the progress and adherence to the agreements. When the UN agreed, bells of peace that seemed so tentative at first sounded long and deeply.

Figure 41 is a Futures wheel-type representation of the Middle East peace process based on the findings of the Millennium Project study.

Figure 41

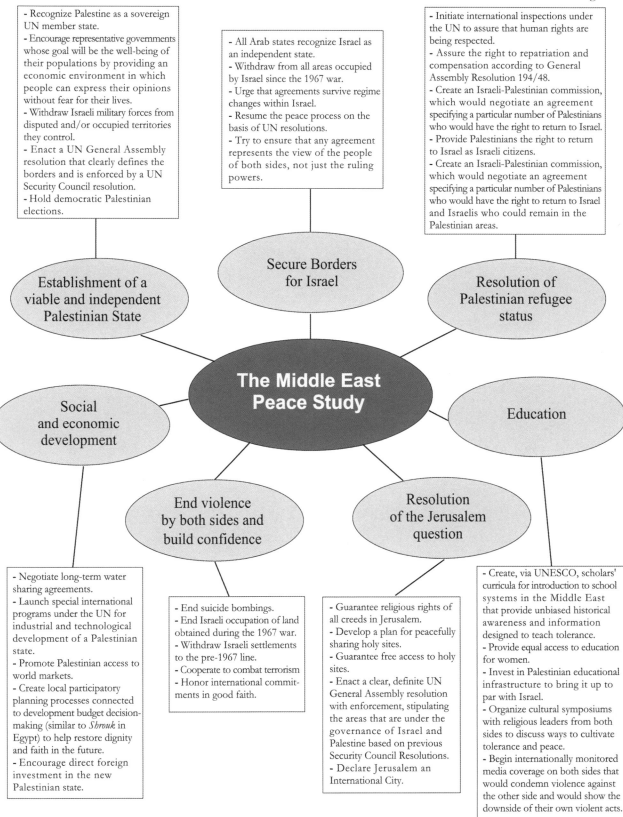

- Recognize Palestine as a sovereign UN member state.
- Encourage representative governments whose goal will be the well-being of their populations by providing an economic environment in which people can express their opinions without fear for their lives.
- Withdraw Israeli military forces from disputed and/or occupied territories they control.
- Enact a UN General Assembly resolution that clearly defines the borders and is enforced by a UN Security Council resolution.
- Hold democratic Palestinian elections.

- All Arab states recognize Israel as an independent state.
- Withdraw from all areas occupied by Israel since the 1967 war.
- Urge that agreements survive regime changes within Israel.
- Resume the peace process on the basis of UN resolutions.
- Try to ensure that any agreement represents the view of the people of both sides, not just the ruling powers.

- Initiate international inspections under the UN to assure that human rights are being respected.
- Assure the right to repatriation and compensation according to General Assembly Resolution 194/48.
- Create an Israeli-Palestinian commission, which would negotiate an agreement specifying a particular number of Palestinians who would have the right to return to Israel.
- Provide Palestinians the right to return to Israel as Israeli citizens.
- Create an Israeli-Palestinian commission, which would negotiate an agreement specifying a particular number of Palestinians who would have the right to return to Israel and Israelis who could remain in the Palestinian areas.

Establishment of a viable and independent Palestinian State

Secure Borders for Israel

Resolution of Palestinian refugee status

The Middle East Peace Study

Social and economic development

Education

End violence by both sides and build confidence

Resolution of the Jerusalem question

- Negotiate long-term water sharing agreements.
- Launch special international programs under the UN for industrial and technological development of a Palestinian state.
- Promote Palestinian access to world markets.
- Create local participatory planning processes connected to development budget decision-making (similar to *Shrouk* in Egypt) to help restore dignity and faith in the future.
- Encourage direct foreign investment in the new Palestinian state.

- End suicide bombings.
- End Israeli occupation of land obtained during the 1967 war.
- Withdraw Israeli settlements to the pre-1967 line.
- Cooperate to combat terrorism
- Honor international commitments in good faith.

- Guarantee religious rights of all creeds in Jerusalem.
- Develop a plan for peacefully sharing holy sites.
- Guarantee free access to holy sites.
- Enact a clear, definite UN General Assembly resolution with enforcement, stipulating the areas that are under the governance of Israel and Palestine based on previous Security Council Resolutions.
- Declare Jerusalem an International City.

- Create, via UNESCO, scholars' curricula for introduction to school systems in the Middle East that provide unbiased historical awareness and information designed to teach tolerance.
- Provide equal access to education for women.
- Invest in Palestinian educational infrastructure to bring it up to par with Israel.
- Organize cultural symposiums with religious leaders from both sides to discuss ways to cultivate tolerance and peace.
- Begin internationally monitored media coverage on both sides that would condemn violence against the other side and would show the downside of their own violent acts.

6.
EMERGING ENVIRONMENTAL SECURITY ISSUES FOR INTERNATIONAL TREATIES

Environmental security is becoming recognized as an important policy framework to improve human security. Although complex in scope, environmental security is becoming a less amorphous concept.

The Millennium Project defines environmental security as environmental viability for life support, with three sub-elements:

- preventing or repairing military damage to the environment,
- preventing or responding to environmentally caused conflicts, and
- protecting the environment due to the moral value of the environment itself.

To make the world a safer place, ensure sustainability, and reverse the trend of environmental degradation, scholars and decisionmakers are examining the links between environment and security, the environmental risk factors that might trigger political tension, and the key players and their actions in order to achieve these goals.

Over the past two years, with financial support from the U.S. Army Environmental Policy Institute, the Millennium Project has been scanning a variety of sources to identify emerging environmental issues with treaty and military implications. The purpose of the study is to give early warning about international environmental issues that could trigger new or change existing international agreements that could have military implications. Over 200 items have been identified. The full text of these items and their sources can be found on the CD in Chapter 9.1, "Emerging Environmental Security Issues."

General patterns and insights from the items identified include:

- "Business as Usual" will be a misleading forecast: New sensor technologies, increasing environmental awareness, and international agreements mean that many actions accepted over the past 10–20 years will not be tolerated over the next decade or two.

- There will be an increasing role for the military in documenting military chemicals, food, equipment, and impacts and locations of weapons (such as the spent uranium shelling controversy); in securing pathogens and toxins from terrorists; in conducting more sophisticated post-conflict cleanups; and in anticipating disasters as their impact and number rise and as disasters become more acute due to climate change and chemical and biological pollution.

- Environmental causes of conflicts are expected to become more significant as environmental deterioration increases the number of "environmental refugees," which will increase the number and scale of conflicts related to migration.

- Environmental issues continue to rise on the international political agenda. (UN Legal Counsel Hans Corell called for more attention to environmental issues than to armed conflicts; UNEP opened a post-conflict, early warning unit and may open an environment and conflict unit.)

- The Aarhus Convention reinforces the growing trend of increased public and NGO participation in shaping national, regional, and international policy, legislation, and treaties.

- Sovereignty and environmental security may increasingly be in conflict.

- Global warming is not going away, and legal mechanisms to recover damages seem inevitable.

- A global framework for chemical, nuclear, and biological waste management is needed.

It is clear that environmental issues are moving higher on the agenda of governments, corporations, international organizations, NGOs, universities, media, private institutions, and individuals around the world. Environmental security has to consider the impacts of new kinds of weapons, asymmetrical conflicts, increasing demands on natural resources, urbanization (which makes more people dependent on vulnerable public utilities), continued advances in environmental law with escalating environmental litigation, and the globalization that is increasing interdependency. Environmental security is one of three fundamental points to be considered for an international charter on values to be submitted to the United Nations. The May 2004 conference on Environmental Security in the 21st Century aimed to find integrated, science-based, diplomatic, and legal solutions for increasing environmental security.

Preventing or Repairing Military Damage to the Environment

The cost of military operations complying with environmental regulations may become so high that the nature of conflict and of the operations themselves could change. Some NATO countries are making considerable effort to introduce new military techniques and equipment in order to minimize environmental damage during conflicts.

One of the most serious issues in post-conflict situations is the long-term environmental degradation partially caused by the collapse of local and national governance. "While humankind's ability to wage war continues apace with new and even more potentially devastating weapons," said Klaus Töpfer, Executive Director of UNEP, "international rules and laws designed to minimize the impact on the Earth's life support system have lagged far behind." The Geneva Protocol's requirement to prevent "widespread, long-term and severe damage" has rendered it ineffective for environmental protection, as it applies only to "expected damages, rather than possible ones" and remains unenforceable due to a lack of a common definition of these three terms and lack of any assessment envisioned to be carried out after a conflict. UNEP recently opened a new post-conflict assessment unit, however, and "crimes against the environment" is on the list of war crimes against Saddam Hussein, separate from financial reparation actions previously taken.

Preventive actions and a timely response are vital in addressing conflict-induced environmental damage. NATO is creating a special chemical, biological, radiological, and nuclear defense unit capable of quick deployment, and it has been suggested that the UN Monitoring, Inspection and Verification Commission (which searched for weapons of mass destruction in Iraq prior to the war) become a permanent agency to investigate biological and missile programs worldwide.

There is an international consensus that the "polluter has to pay," with no exemption for the military. Governments are increasingly likely to be held accountable for hazards from abandoned weapons, even those from as far back as World War II. Since the UN has been consistent in recent years in its interest in long-term and widespread contamination issues, it is reasonable to expect international agreements to address this issue. A Geneva Convention for the Environment is needed that clearly lays out environmental impact standards during military conflicts.

How severe do environmental impacts have to become in one country to allow others to intervene in order to prevent more serious environmentally caused conflicts or long-term environmental damage? The prognosis of several Global Challenges in Chapter 1 plus increasing globalization and the proliferation of international environmental agreements mean that environmental security, national interests, and sovereignty are likely to be increasingly in conflict. New agreements and protocols are needed to prevent ad hoc decisions in these areas.

New technologies should be considered for designing cleaner warfare, detecting and cleaning up contaminated sites, and improving the planning of military operations to minimize environmental harm. Software algorithms for ecoterrorism prediction and simulations might improve environmental policy efforts by identifying plausible futures linked to key environmental issues. DARPA estimates that within two years, humans and computers might "think together" in real time to "anticipate and preempt terrorist threats." Virtual Earth simulation using real-world terrain databases will also help reduce the environmental impact of military operations.

This trend will be enhanced by the increasing ability of nanotechnology to produce tiny, intelligent pieces of equipment. Robots significantly reduce logistical requirements, which translate into lighter environmental footprints and reduce the amount of battlefield waste.

Smart dust has been in development for the last decade with the intent of providing a cheap, lightweight, lingering, swarm-based technology that could provide multispectral intelligence over critical battlefield and post-conflict areas inaccessible or too hostile for other reconnaissance technologies. Nanoscale equipment could detect chemical warfare agents and reduce toxic chemicals and heavy metals into less toxic compounds. "Intelligent" networks based on microsensor arrays connected to artificial neural networks have the potential to provide an early warning of chemical warfare agents well before concentration levels become lethal. Antibody-based sensors can detect a bioterrorist attack in real time and can distinguish among different pathogens.

Transgenic plants could help decontaminate the environment by detecting and selectively destroying or segregating hazardous or polluting elements. Genetically modified animals might also one day be used for reconnaissance or cleanup.

However, new technologies could also trigger new forms of arms race. Gamma-ray weapons would be capable of killing any living thing in the immediate area, and any undetonated isomer could be a somewhat "dirty" bomb. New lethal viruses and artificial viruses that could lead to a new life form have already been created. The Human Epigenome Project could lead to a potential genetics arms race.

Scientific and health communities are considering how to handle the problems of genetically modified viruses and pathogenic chimeras. WHO's committee on smallpox research is currently weighing various proposals for new and continuing experimental efforts. It is likely that discussions on biosafety and biodefense will soon move from the health and research committees to wider international legislative bodies, triggering new protocols to existing treaties (such as the Biological and Toxin Weapons Convention) or even to new international treaties that deal with genetic manipulation and its hazards.

Preventing or Responding to Environmentally Caused Conflicts

Environmental degradation causes more refugees than war and politics do. Although so far the Office of the UN High Commissioner for Refugees does not consider "environmental refugee" as a category under the Geneva Convention, the sheer number of displaced persons uprooted by environmental damage underscores the need to take environmental security far more seriously. Convention Plus, a new UNHCR initiative that is focused on increased use of comprehensive and regional approaches to preventing and resolving refugee situations and other forms of involuntary displacement, does not exclude environmentally induced displacement, however. Lester Brown, President of the Earth Policy Institute, in analyzing the movements of environmental refugees and the relationship of such migrations to national security, argues that a global effort is needed to address the causes of these environmentally driven migrations.

A UNEP survey found that links between the environment and poverty, trade, and conflict were the main "knowledge gaps" in understanding environmentally related issues. As a result, "UNEP might set up a new secretariat on environmental peace and conflict," said Dr. Steve Lonergan, Director of UNEP's division of Early Warnings and Assessment.

Case studies suggest that the major sources of civil conflict associated with the availability of cropland and fresh water have been generated by the decreasing capacity of rural areas to maintain secure livelihoods and absorb growing labor forces. In the past, eruptions of civil tensions over cropland have been more common than those over freshwater resources. While low per capita levels of land and water persist in several populous industrial countries, these countries—with robust urban economies and well-run services—are much less vulnerable to civil conflict involving these resources. Tensions between states over renewable natural resources have most often developed over rights to ocean fisheries and transboundary freshwater supplies and have generally led to interstate negotiations rather than warfare. Continued rapid population growth in the developing world, however, suggests a future unlike the past.

Food shortages induced by elevated temperatures and aquifer depletions are increasing worldwide. If such environmental conditions continue, the world will soon be unable to feed itself. According to the Earth Policy Institute, the global 2003 harvest fell short of consumption by 93 million tons. Grain harvest shortfalls may drive conflicts in areas already unstable. FAO has highlighted 35 countries now facing serious food shortages; two dozen of these are in Africa.

About 40% of humanity lives in one of the 260 major international water basins shared by two or more countries; however, the prospects for continued interstate cooperation, particularly over transboundary water rights, remain uncertain. Freshwater responsible management and an increase of bilateral and multilateral treaties are keys to preventing conflict in some areas. The designation of 2003 as the International Year of Freshwater inspired worldwide events designed to promote more responsible water use and conservation. UN's International Decade "Water for Life," in 2005–15, will also draw attention to the implementation of water projects around the world. Predictive conflict modeling should be used to determine conflict high-risk areas and to improve policy for enhancing stability in those countries and should be made available to the public.

Protecting the Environment Due to Its Inherent Moral Value

The first three Challenges in Chapter 1 address a range of forecasts and strategies relevant to protecting the environment. Increased awareness among governments, local authorities, industry, and civil society with regard to the environment is leading to the expansion of environmentally sound practices for the protection of the environment. Enhanced cooperation between governments, coordinated by regional and international organizations, contributes significantly to improving the environment through multilateral agreements.

Currently there are about 300 multilateral environment-related international treaties, conventions, and protocols, according to Worldwatch Institute. UNEP reports that over the last two years governments signed or ratified 15 global and regional international environmental legal instruments. The key agreements related to environmental security that were recently adopted or amended or that are pending are as follows; further details can be found in Chapter 9 on the CD:

- Rotterdam Convention on the Prior Informed Consent Procedure for Certain Hazardous Chemicals and Pesticides in International Trade
- Stockholm Convention on Persistent Organic Pollutants
- Cartagena Protocol on Biosafety
- Protocol on Heavy Metals
- New resolutions on nuclear, chemical, and biological weapons
- Global classification and labeling system for chemicals
- Kyoto Protocol, pending Russia ratification
- Montreal Protocol (on ozone depletion)— "critical use exemptions" granted but Klaus Töpfer has called on nations "to speed up the development and spread of ozone-friendly replacements"

- Phaseout of single-hull tankers—amendments to the International Convention for the Prevention of Pollution from Ships expected in April 2005
- International Convention for the Control and Management of Ships' Ballast Water and Sediments (adopted and in force when 30 states representing 35% of world merchant shipping tonnage ratify)
- Regional water management agreements
- International legal instruments for mountain regions
- Conventions for regional protection (such as northern Pacific Ocean, the Carpathians, and the Caspian Sea)
- Protocol on Strategic Environmental Assessment (to the UNECE Convention on Environmental Impact Assessment in a Transboundary Context)
- ASEAN Agreement on Transboundary Haze Pollution
- Protocol on Shared Watercourse Systems in the Southern African Development Community
- Protocol amending the Andean Subregional Integration Agreement (Cartagena Agreement)
- Protocol on Persistent Organic Pollutants, the sixth to take effect under UNECE's Geneva Convention on Long-range Transboundary Air Pollution

An integrated data and information system of all major environmental observing facilities (based on land, on sea, and in space) will be useful to detect possible hot spots and to enforce environmental agreements. Representatives from 47 countries at the Earth Observation Summit in Tokyo in April 2004 approved measures and goals for an observation network to be in operation by 2015. It will cover all environment-related aspects—from natural disasters and human-induced hazards to improving management of natural resources.

International harmonized standard systems and agreements for better information sharing and integration, along with a global and comprehensive database with systematic assessment of national and regional environmental situations and trends, are essential for efficient enforcement. UNEP notes an increased participation by industry in the adoption of voluntary standards that take into account environmental considerations. OECD members have agreed to strengthen environmental standards for companies bidding on contracts to build civil infrastructure projects around the world with funding from export credit agencies. Several regional organizations developed their own standards and databases to assess compliance with multilateral environmental agreements.

Although many laboratory biosafety standards exist, there is no international treaty governing their usage and there is no uniformity of application or compliance requirements. Bioscientists from around the world began discussions on establishing international biosecurity measures along with standards and protocols that would lead to improved security of facilities conducting infectious disease research worldwide. The UN Security Council increased its role in preventing terrorist access to weapons of mass destruction by unanimously adopting in April 2004 a binding resolution criminalizing the production or acquisition of weapons of mass destruction by non-state actors. The recently launched Strategic Approach to International Chemicals Management addresses the widening gap among countries in following chemical safety policies.

The health and environmental implications of nanotechnology and other new technologies should be addressed by legally binding mecha-

nisms, ethical and legal standards, and defensive technologies. The Canada-based ETC Group is collaborating with other partners to develop an International Convention for the Evaluation of New Technologies, which it hopes to submit to the United Nations in 2004.

It is estimated that the rate of loss of biodiversity is the highest in human history. The UN Seventh Conference of the Parties of the Convention on Biological Diversity, which met in February 2004, reaffirmed governments' commitment to establish a worldwide network of protected areas (on land by 2010 and in oceans by 2012) by setting rigorous targets to reduce loss of biological diversity.

The Cartagena Protocol on Biosafety entered into force in September 2003; it aims to protect biological diversity from the potential risks that may be posed by living modified organisms or genetically modified organisms by adopting strict procedures for labeling, handling, transporting, packaging, and identifying GMOs. A negotiating group of experts will address the issue of liability and redress for damages resulting from transboundary movements of GMOs and will develop a regime by 2008. New legislation expected to come into force in September 2004 requires each variety of GMO used in food and animal feed to be assigned a unique code for accurate labeling and traceability and sets the accidental mixing of GM in non-GM biological materials at no more than 0.9%. The new regulation also allows EU states to set "appropriate measures" that protect conventional strains from cross-pollinating with GM crops.

New initiatives to increase eco-efficiency and eco-security are continuing to emerge all over the world and at all levels—the UN, regional groups, and national and local organizations. See Chapter 9 in the CD for more information.

File   Edit   View   Favorites   Tools   Help

Address   http://www.mpweblogs.org/MP-EWS   Go

MILLENNIUM PROJECT ENVIRONMENTAL SCANNING WEBLOG & DATABASE

HOME | ABOUT | ARCHIVES | LINKS | CONTACT

2004 State of the Future

Jerome C. Glenn & Theodore J. Gordon

Friday, June 11, 2004

MP Nodes Collaborate to Produce New Global Change Weblog & Database

In cooperation with the Kuwait Node and Dar Almashora, the Millennium Project has developed a unique early warning system for the Kuwait Oil Company using open source software to create a weblog datab...

Members:
Login | Register | Member List

About this Weblog & Database

There are many methods for exploring prospects for the future, but probably the most fundamental method to support ... ...search is the use of a

90

7.

MILLENNIUM PROJECT ENVIRONMENTAL SCANNING WEBLOG DATABASE

There are many methods for exploring prospects for the future, but probably the most fundamental way to support futures research is using a system to identify developments that promise change and to keep track of changes that are under way. Such a system is referred to as an early warning or environmental scanning system. The term "environmental" in this case does not refer to nature but to the "environment" being scanned for change. This could be the social, political, technological, or economic as well as the natural environment. (For an overview of environmental scanning, see Chapter 2, Futures Research Methodology, Version 2.0, available at www.acunu.org/millennium/FRM-v2.html.)

In cooperation with the Kuwait Node and the consulting company Dar Almashora, the Millennium Project has developed a unique early warning system for the Kuwait Oil Company using open source software to create a weblog with some database elements. A weblog is a log or collection of text, graphics, and so on usually copied from Web pages to a Web site that allows the user to manage this information in various ways. Millennium Project participants can select part or all of a Web page or can create new content, save it in a weblog, add information relevant to the item, and invite others to comment.

Working with the Maui Cyber Node and the German Node, the Millennium Project is creating a variation of this system to monitor global change in order to update and improve the 15 Global Challenges and the State of the Future Index. As an evolving collective intelligence, the Project plans to continue experimentation with new systems. In the meantime, readers are welcome to explore the current status of the Millennium Project ESS Weblog and Database (see Figure 42) via a link at www.stateofthefuture.org.

Items can be entered into this weblog and database by the Project's staff, by Node Chairs, and by participants in the Project's research who are registered on the Web site. Attached to the entry form for the information copied into the weblog are the fields for the database. The fields allow a person to indicate which Global Challenge is relevant, the significance or importance to the Challenge, potential consequences or impacts to the future of the world in general, the key actors regarding the information, the current status of the information, and other comments that are vital for understanding the future significance of the information. The use of these fields allows computer-generated reports to help find emerging patterns.

A person might generate a report of all the entries under actors and then determine if any patterns exist. In this way, additional "weak signals" or new elements might be found within the pattern of previously identified issues, trends, or potential future events. Registered participants can subscribe to e-mail "watch lists" on the weblog, select syndicated headlines, and keep track of futures activities via a calendar. The diagram in Figure 43 shows the information flow and feedback system to contribute to the growing collective intelligence about the Global Challenges.

Comments on the entries can be made by anyone (with editorial oversight). From time to time, Project staff, Node Chairs, and Project interns will review the entries for significance to

Current Status of the Front Page of the Weblog Database

Figure 42

the 15 Global Challenges and then will place the results of that analysis into a knowledge base tailored to support the Challenge updating process. This will result in an ongoing feedback system to increase the collective intelligence of the Millennium Project.

Ideally, a dynamic knowledge repository will be constructed, drawing on the weblog as a key source. It would be a unified and logically structured form that can evolve with the cumulative research and wisdom of the Project.

Initially it would be organized around the 15 Global Challenges, SOFI, and any special research topics (such as the Middle East peace scenario study, global management issues for science and technology, or environmental security) and would reflect the subtopics and relationships that exist within and among these areas.

Readers are invited to submit new insights to global challenges in the new weblog from any reliable source of information such as journals, organizational press releases, Web sites, and authorities at conferences or key persons known to have reliable insights. The detailed instructions on the use of the database are given in Appendix K on the CD.

Figure 43

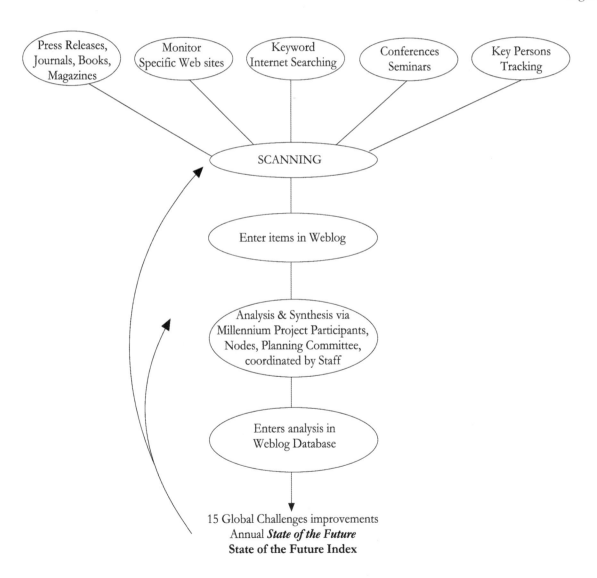

APPENDIX
Millennium Project Participants Demographics

There were 245 futurists, scholars, business planners, scientists, and decisionmakers who contributed this year to the global challenges, the State of the Future Index, the Middle East Peace Scenarios, and the future international environmental security issues study. The graphs below show the regional and sectoral demographics.

Participants in the 2003–04 Program

Total participants: 245

Sectoral Demographic

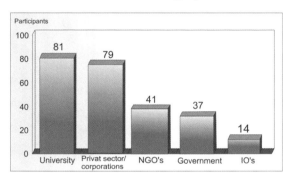

Regional Demographic

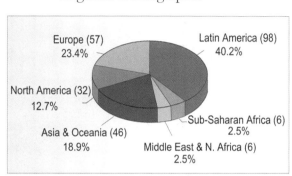

However, much of the work is cumulative in nature, which has come from 1,654 participants over the past seven years. The second set of graphs shows their regional and sectoral demographics.

Participants Since 1996

Total participants: 1,651

Sectoral Demographic

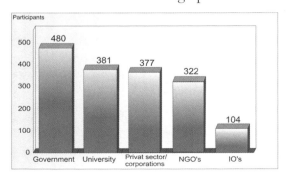

Regional Demographic

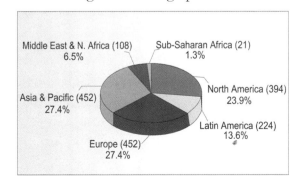

ACRONYMS AND ABBREVIATIONS

AC/UNU	American Council for the United Nations University
ASEAN	Association of Southeast Asian Nations
BBC	British Broadcasting Corporation
B2B	business-to-business
CDC	Centers for Disease Control and Prevention (US)
CEDAW	Convention on the Elimination of Discrimination Against Women
CNN	Cable News Network
CO_2	carbon dioxide
DARPA	Defense Advanced Research Projects Agency
ESS	environmental scanning system
EU	European Union
FAO	Food and Agriculture Organization of the UN
GDP	gross domestic product
GMOs	genetically modified organisms
HDI	Human Development Index
IAEA	International Atomic Energy Agency
ICC	International Criminal Court
ICT	information and communications technology
IDC	International Data Corp
IEA	International Energy Agency
ISO	International Organization for Standardization
IMF	International Monetary Fund
ITU	International Telecommunications Union
LQ	lower quartile
MDG	Millennium Development Goal
MIT	Massachusetts Institute of Technology
NAFTA	North American Free Trade Agreement
NATO	North Atlantic Treaty Organization
NBIC	nanotechnology, biotechnology, information technology, and cognitive science
NGO	nongovernmental organization
OECD	Organisation for Economic Co-operation and Development
PC	personal computer
PLO	Palestine Liberation Organization
ppm	parts per million
PPP	purchasing power parity
R&D	research and development
RLP	Religious Leaders for Peace*
S&T	science and technology
SOFI	State of the Future Index
TIA	trend impact analysis
TOC	transnational organized crime

UK	United Kingdom
UN	United Nations
UNDP	United Nations Development Programme
UNECE	UN Economic Commission for Europe
UNEP	United Nations Environment Programme
UNESCO	UN Educational, Scientific, and Cultural Organization
UQ	upper quartile
UNHCR	United Nations High Commissioner for Refugees
UNSCO	UN Special Coordinator's Office*
US	United States
USAID	US Agency for International Development
USSR	Union of Soviet Socialist Republics
WHO	World Health Organization
WMD	weapons of mass destruction
WSSD	World Summit on Sustainable Development
WTO	World Trade Organization

*Terms used in scenarios for the Middle East in Chapter 5.